THE SECRET OF
Contentment

THE SECRET OF
Contentment

JUANITA PURCELL

REGULAR BAPTIST PRESS
1300 North Meacham Road
Schaumburg, Illinois 60173-4806

Special Thanks

A special thanks to Lenore Igleheart for all the hours she saved me in preparing this book for publication. During the time I was discipling Lenore, I discovered she had computer skills and she agreed to type this book for me. She diligently deciphered the scribbling in my notes with a happy, contented spirit.

THE SECRET OF CONTENTMENT
© 2006 Regular Baptist Press • Schaumburg, Illinois
All rights reserved • Printed in U.S.A.
www.RegularBaptistPress.org • 1-800-727-4440
RBP5353 • ISBN 978-1-59402-425-2

Third Printing—2009

Contents

10. Read Isaiah 55:8 and 9. Why can't we always understand God's sovereign rule in our lives?

God is often silent when we prefer that he speak, and he interrupts us when we prefer that he stay silent. His ways are not our ways. To live with the sacred God of creation means that we conduct our lives with a God who does not explain himself to us. It means that we worship a God who is often mysterious—too mysterious to fit our formulas for better living.[2]

---

11. Read James 1:13, Isaiah 45:5–7, and Psalm 76:10. James tells us that God is not the author of evil. What do the verses in Isaiah 45 and Psalm 76 tell us?

We must, therefore, conclude that God neither causes sin, incites it, authorizes it, or approves it. He does, however, permit it by allowing creatures, whom He has endowed with a moral will, to rebel against His authority. He then sovereignly overrules their evil to accomplish His sovereign predetermined purposes. In the allowance of evil, God demonstrates how great He really is. Or as Joseph so accurately articulated when giving his analysis of the evil done to him by his brothers who sold him into slavery, "You meant evil against me, but God meant it for good in order to bring about this present result, to preserve many people alive" (Genesis 50:20).[3]

---

7. First Timothy 6:15 has helped me accept God's sovereignty in my life. What does this verse teach you?

The Old Testament tells about a potentate named Nebuchadnezzar. This king set himself up as the supreme ruler of his kingdom, but he also wanted to control people's lives. He made a ninety-foot tall golden idol and demanded that everyone bow down and worship it. God made Nebuchadnezzar insane to humble him and to bring him to the place where he knew that "the most High ruleth in the kingdom of men, and giveth it to whomsoever he will" (Daniel 4:32). The king lived like an animal for seven years.

8. Read Daniel 4:34–37. After God humbled King Nebuchadnezzar, how did he view God?

Nebuchadnezzar's reasoning did not return to him until he started thinking right about God (Daniel 4:37). We also need to think right about God and see Him as the blessed "King of kings, and Lord of lords" (1 Timothy 6:15).

9. Many people rebel against the idea of a sovereign God ruling their lives. All they want is a jack-in-the-box God. What kind of God is that?

5. What do the following verses teach us about God's sovereignty?

Proverbs 16:9

Ecclesiastes 7:13

Psalm 115:3

Daniel 4:34 and 35

Lamentations 3:37 and 38

Confidence in the sovereignty of God in all that affects us is crucial to our trusting Him. If there is a single event in all of the universe that can occur outside of God's sovereign control then we cannot trust Him. His love may be infinite, but if His power is limited and His purpose can be thwarted, we cannot trust Him.[1]

First Timothy 6:15 says, "Which in his times he shall [show], who is the blessed and only Potentate, the King of kings, and Lord of lords." A potentate, or sovereign, rules his or her realm.

6. "Potentate" means "ruler" or "sovereign." How does 1 Timothy 6:15 describe our sovereign God?

You must *receive* Jesus Christ as your Savior before you can personally experience His love for you and the abundant life He has planned for you.

> *"For by grace are ye saved through faith"*
> *(Ephesians 2:8).*

You can receive Christ right now by an act of *faith*.

Are you ready to believe on Christ as your Savior? Use the following prayer as a guide to help you express your desire to God: "Lord Jesus, I know I am a sinner and need Your forgiveness. I believe You died for my sins. Right now I open the door of my life and receive You as my Savior and Lord. Take control of my life; replace all the restlessness and anxiety with peace and contentment."

We cannot have the peace *of* God, which leads to contentment, until we experience peace *with* God through salvation. I trust you have taken time to consider it and have responded in a positive way. If you believed on Jesus as your Savior, be sure to tell your Bible study leader or another friend.

Peace of God

We have peace *with* God when we receive Christ as our Savior. We enjoy the peace *of* God as we learn to trust Him with our lives. Are you experiencing the peace of God? If not, could it be that you have never really accepted God's divine sovereignty in your life and circumstances?

4. Look up the word "sovereign" in a dictionary and write down the definition.

The sovereignty of God means God is God; He has no equal (Isaiah 40:25). He does whatever He pleases with His creation because all of it belongs to Him. Psalm 24:1 says, "The earth is the LORD's, and the fulness thereof; the world, and they that dwell therein."

2. Describe how a person can have peace with God. Read Ephesians 2:13 and 14 and Romans 5:1.

3. Are you a restless, discontented person with no peace? Do you want peace with God? If you answered yes, read the verses below that explain how you can have peace with God.

> *"For God so loved the world, that he gave his only begotten Son, that whosoever believeth in him should not perish, but have everlasting life" (John 3:16).*

> *"I am come that they might have life, and that they might have it more abundantly" (John 10:10).*

God *loves* you and wants you to enjoy the *abundant life* He offers you.

> *"For all have sinned, and come short of the glory of God" (Romans 3:23).*

> *"For the wages of sin is death [that is, separation from God]" (Romans 6:23).*

People are *sinful*, and their sin *separates* them from God.

> *"But God commendeth his love toward us, in that, while we were yet sinners, Christ died for us" (Romans 5:8).*

> *"Jesus saith unto him, I am the way, the truth, and the life: no man cometh unto the Father, but by me" (John 14:6).*

The death of Jesus Christ is the only *provision* God has made to pay for people's sin.

> *"But as many as received him, to them gave he power to become the sons of God, even to them that believe on his name" (John 1:12).*

Searching for Contentment

"But our God is in the heavens: he hath done whatsoever he hath pleased" (Psalm 115:3).

If you stood in a busy mall and asked people to answer a question for a survey, would many people stop? Probably not. Why? They are too busy or don't want to get involved. If you could get a few of them to answer your question, you might be surprised at their answers. Oh, by the way, I did take a survey. Below are my question and the answers I got.

Question: "What are you searching for in life?"
Answers:
"Happiness and to be successful."
"Money, love, and a normal family life with a happy home."
"Happiness."

Not one person said he or she was searching for peace or contentment. Most people in our materialistic society do not know that the things they are searching for will not bring contentment. I can hear someone saying, "Doesn't happiness bring contentment?" No! Because happiness depends on happenings, such as having money, it can be here today and gone tomorrow. Contentment is built on a relationship with Christ—a solid foundation that never changes. So how do people find contentment?

Peace with God

Contentment starts with peace with God. We receive this peace when we accept Christ as Savior.

1. How does the Bible picture people before they are saved? Read Isaiah 57:20 and 21 and Romans 3:17.

Preface

A wise person once said, "Discontentment makes rich people poor. Contentment makes poor people rich." My prayer is that this study will lead you to a contented life, if you do not already experience it. When you find contentment, you will realize you have found something the richest person cannot buy. You will discover that contentment is a state of the heart that does not fluctuate with circumstances or people. Ultimately, we will discover that contentment is more a change of our attitude than a change in our circumstances. Are you ready to find the Biblical secrets to contentment? Let's get started!

It is hard for us to fathom that a God of love permits the death of a mate or a child, cancer, or the loss of a job. Did God allow all of Job's adversities and calamities (see Job 1)? Yes! Job 1:12 reveals that God gave Satan permission to test Job.

12. How do we know Job understood that God allowed his trials and controlled his circumstances (Job 1:20, 21)?

13. Did Job ever fully comprehend why God allowed all his trials? What did he understand (Job 42:2, 3)?

Faith submits, taking God at His word and resting in His character. Can you see that this Sovereign One Who sits upon the throne of the universe is just, merciful, holy, righteous—a God of love? Rest and listen.[4]

---

14. Abraham called God "the Judge of all the earth" (Genesis 18:25). What is the main responsibility of a judge?

15. Read Genesis 18:25 and Psalm 145:17. What kind of judge is handing down the verdicts in our lives?

Psalm 106:1 says, "Praise ye the LORD. O give thanks unto the LORD, for he is good: for his mercy endureth for ever."

16. When are we most likely to say, "God is so good"? When are we least likely to say this?

17. What is happening in your life right now that makes you think, *God isn't good, or He wouldn't have allowed this*? How could this situation work for your spiritual good?

18. Our thoughts and motives are often focused toward a comfortable life. What is God always thinking about those who love Him (Romans 8:28, 29)?

God's working in our lives could be compared to baking a cake.

> *"Some ingredients of a cake taste good by themselves. Other ingredients taste terrible by themselves: nutmeg, baking soda, etc. But when you mix those things together and get the mixer churning, the good and the bad blend and turn out for the better. When that cake comes out of the oven, the good and the bad have been so mixed, so integrated that they have produced something well worth the waiting.*[5]

God takes all the good and all the bad experiences in our lives to help conform us to the likeness of His Son, Jesus Christ.

Have you been wrestling with the question, Why, God? Can

you change your question to, How, God? How can I grow spiritually from this experience and bring honor to Your name? Coming
to grips with God's sovereign control in my life has taught me to
live a palms-up life.

19. What is your concept of a palms-up life?

20. What relationship does palms-up living have with content-
    ment (Job 23:14; Psalms 115:3; 135:6)?

---

*We will probably spend most of our life with family,
friends, good health and good work. But they are
not ours by rights. They are not promised to us. We
may have to give them back to God at any moment.
Someday we will give them back. The trick is to learn
how to do that before they leave us. That allows us
to spend the rest of our time enjoying them as the
temporary gifts that they are.*[6]

Accepting the sovereignty of God in your life will help you in
your search for contentment.

 ## *From My Heart*

For me, finding the secret of contentment started with living
a palms-up life. Palms-up living was a slow process that occurred
in my life over a period of a few years. I remember the day the
process started. I had taught a Bible study on Romans 8:28 and
29 that day. For the first time I came to the full realization that
all the good and all the bad that had happened in my life were for
one ultimate purpose: that I might become more like Jesus Christ
(Romans 8:29). I got down on my knees and told the Lord, "If

Your goal for my life is to be more like Your Son, then I want that as the life-long goal of my life as well."

Since that day, I daily (mentally and sometimes literally) put my palms up before the Lord and say, "Give what You want and take what You want." When I first started saying that to the Lord, I was fearful of what He might take from me. One day I realized I must give Him everything I have; then He couldn't take it from me. From that day on, I have visualized placing every person and everything in my life at the feet of Jesus and saying, "It all belongs to You." Never again have I feared He might take something from me, because I have already given it to Him. Palms-up living has taught me what contentment really is: total trust in my sovereign God.

From Your Heart

Have you been struggling with God's sovereignty in your life? Did you learn anything in this lesson that helped you? What was it? Have you tried palms-up living?

Notes

1. Jerry Bridges, *Trusting God* (Colorado Springs: NavPress, 1988), 37.

2. M. Craig Barnes, *When God Interrupts* (Downers Grove, IL: InterVarsity Press, 1996), 135.

3. Tony Evans, *Our God Is Awesome* (Chicago: Moody Press, 1994), 99, 100.

4. Kay Arthur, *The Sovereignty of God* (Chattanooga: Precept Ministries, 1987), 11.

5. Evans, 100, 101.

6. Barnes, 18.

Faith: The First Factor in Finding Contentment

"But without faith it is impossible to please him: for he that cometh to God must believe that he is, and that he is a rewarder of them that diligently seek him" (Hebrews 11:6).

Faith is the bridge we must all pass over to please God and be pleased with God. "Without faith it is impossible to please him" (Hebrews 11:6). The Children of Israel are a vivid picture of people who didn't please God and weren't pleased with Him. What was their basic problem? A lack of faith.

The Israelites had seen God perform miracle after miracle, yet they didn't trust Him. They missed going into the land flowing with milk and honey and wandered in the wilderness for forty years because of their lack of faith. "And the LORD said unto Moses, How long will this people provoke me? and how long will it be ere they believe me, for all the signs which I have [shown] among them? I will smite them with the pestilence, and disinherit them" (Numbers 14:11, 12).

The Basis for Our Faith

Have you been living in a wilderness of discontent? Could it be that you, like the Children of Israel, have been living a life of murmuring and complaining because you won't trust God? Has God been whispering or maybe even shouting in your ear, "How long will you provoke Me because you won't believe Me?" Remember, you cannot please God or be pleased with God without faith.

1. How do you define faith?

2. What is God's definition of faith in Hebrews 11:1?

Faith must be based on substance or certainty.

3. Where do we find the facts to give us a certain and secure faith, according to Romans 10:17?

> *Many people are willing to believe regarding those things that seem probable to them. Faith has nothing to do with probabilities. The province of faith begins where probabilities cease and sight and sense fail. Appearances are not to be taken into account. The question is—whether God has spoken it in His Word.*[1]

4. If you have been born again, on what facts did you base your faith (1 Corinthians 15:1–4)?

We began our spiritual life by faith, and it continues by faith. "As ye have therefore received Christ Jesus the Lord, so walk ye in him" (Colossians 2:6).

5. What are we to do *in the faith* (1 Corinthians 16:13)?

What are we to do *by faith* (2 Corinthians 5:7)?

What are we to do *by the faith* of the Son of God (Galatians 2:20)?

6. God wants us to walk by faith. How would we rather walk (2 Corinthians 5:7)?

Learning to walk with God is a process. And just when we think we have it all figured out, God leads us into a new place where our old tricks won't work. In fact, it may seem like we're learning how to walk all over again. And in a way we are. We enter unfamiliar territory and are soon reminded that, on our own, we stumble. Yet when we take His hand, we fly. God wants us to soar above the limitations of our lives and ourselves. He wants to take us to a place we have never been before and can't get to from where we are without His help.[2]

How Faith Grows and Stabilizes

7. Read 1 Peter 2:2. God pictures us as newborn babes when we are saved, or born again. How would *you* describe a new believer's faith?

8. When our faith is weak and immature, we experience many up-and-down times. How does James 1:6–8 describe this kind of faith?

We could compare a new believer's faith to a child who needs training wheels on her bike to keep her from falling. She needs a lot of support and encouragement from others holding her up.

As a Christian woman matures in faith, she removes the training wheels. Her faith stabilizes when, instead of expecting others to hold her up, she fixes her eyes on Christ. As David wrote in Psalm 25:15, "Mine eyes are ever toward the LORD." A settled, steady faith will carry us in the good times and the bad times.

9. A mature level of faith is unwavering or unshakable. Name some Bible characters who reached this level of faith (Habakkuk 3:1, 2, 17–19; Job 1:1; 13:15; 23:10; 42:2; Jeremiah 1:1, 2; 20:7–9; 31:3; 32:17).

10. What was the basis for their unshakable faith (Proverbs 3:5)?

As Rabbi Abraham Heschel observed, "Faith like Job's cannot be shaken because it is the result of having been shaken." . . . Job saw the darkest side of life, heard the deepest silence of God, and still believed.[3]

---

11. What is your level of faith?

____ Immature and unstable

____ Steady

____ Unwavering or unshakable

12. Has God been testing your faith lately? Is He moving you to a new level of faith? What is happening in your life, and how are you responding?

> *Don't be alarmed. Remember your walk is not by sight, but by faith. And it takes only a little bit of faith to reach out for Isaiah 50:10. . . . God agrees with you; there are days when it's hard to see even a single ray of brightness in your circumstances. But even in the darkness, God promises that you will surely find Him. Close. Near. Ever-present.*[4]

This kind of unwavering faith, which allows us to walk in the dark, is based on the *character of God* and the *Word of God*.

The Character of God

> *The ancients were commended for such faith—not for the strength or quantity, but for the focus and object of their faith. They "fixed their eyes" upon the unseen Lord, the "author and [finisher]" of their faith (Heb. 12:2). And we, following their lead, can learn to focus upon the greatness of God, upon His unimpeachable character, and so learn to trust Him in the difficulties of daily life—for He is the Lord of all.*[5]

13. Read Romans 8:28 and 29. Why can unwavering faith trust God's character? What is the ultimate purpose for everything God allows?

14. According to John 10:27 and 28, why can unwavering faith trust God's character?

> *Had we no tests, no great hedged-in experiences, we would never know what a wonderful Deliverer and triumphant Guide we have!*[6]

15. In what area of your life do you find it the most difficult to trust God right now? What aspects of God's character are related to this problem?

The Word of God

When we read God's Word, it lights our path and keeps us surefooted. "Thy Word is a lamp unto my feet, and a light unto my path" (Psalm 119:105) is more than just a line from a nice worship song. It is a way of life. Walking step by step with God can only be done successfully if we have God's footlights showing us the way.[7]

16. Read Matthew 24:35 and 1 Peter 1:25. Why can unwavering faith trust in the Word of God?

17. According to James 1:2–5, why can unwavering faith trust in the Word of God?

18. What aspects of the Word of God are related to the area you are having a hard time trusting God with?

In order to trust God, we must always view our adverse circumstances through the eyes of faith,

> *not of sense. And just as the faith of salvation comes through hearing the message of the gospel (Romans 10:17), so the faith to trust God in adversity comes through the Word of God alone. It is only in the Scriptures that we find an adequate view of God's relationship to and involvement in our painful circumstances. It is only from the Scriptures, applied to our hearts by the Holy Spirit, that we receive the grace to trust God in adversity.*[8]

I trust it is a settled conviction in your heart that faith is rooted in God's character and based on the Word of God, not on feelings. After you have settled this conviction in your heart and mind, you will start making leaps and bounds in your faith. That is when you will start moving toward contentment.

From My Heart

Many people describe faith as a leap in the dark. That's pretty scary! But I have learned that for the child of God, faith is not a leap in the dark. It is walking in the dark with God holding our hands and our eyes fixed on Him. When the darkness veils His lovely face, when I can't hear His voice, when all the Bible promises seem totally false—that is when I must trust in the things He has taught me about *His character* from *His Word.* I must believe that the promises are true and that nothing can separate me from His love (Romans 8:38, 39).

I need more faith and you need more faith. However, we will never have an unshakable faith until we go through circumstances that force us to act by the invisible rather than the visible. Living a palms-up life has helped me learn to walk by faith, not by sight.

Yes, faith is difficult, but we never walk alone. If we are God's children, our sovereign God, Who is in control of everything, walks with us. "Who . . . walketh in darkness, and hath no light? let him trust in the name of the LORD, and [rely] upon his God" (Isaiah 50:10).

From Your Heart

Is God asking you to walk by faith in some particular area? Has He asked you to trust Him with your husband or lack of a husband, a child, a financial crisis, an illness? Are you trusting only in what you can see, or are you trusting in God's Word?

Notes

1. George Mueller, quoted by Miles J. Stanford, *The Complete Green Letters* (Grand Rapids: Zondervan Publishing House, 1983), 4.

2. Stormie Omartian, *Just Enough Light for the Step I'm On* (Eugene, OR: Harvest House Publishers, 1999), 15.

3. Philip Yancey, *Disappointment with God* (Grand Rapids: Zondervan Publishing House, 1988), 208, 210.

4. Joni Eareckson Tada, "Not One Ray of Light," *Moody* (July/August 1992): 32.

5. Penelope Stokes, "The God in Whom We Trust," *Discipleship Journal* (1987): 22.

6. Mrs. Charles E. Cowman, *Springs in the Valley* (Grand Rapids: Zondervan Publishing House, 1968), 108.

7. Omartian, 49.

8. Bridges, 18.

Learning to Be Content

"Not that I speak in respect of want: for I have learned, in whatsoever state I am, therewith to be content" (Philippians 4:11).

The apostle Paul was in prison ("my bonds") when he wrote to the believers at Philippi (Philippians 1:7). He wrote that he had learned to be content in whatever circumstance God put him (4:11).

Paul's Background

Before Paul received Christ as Savior, he lived an affluent lifestyle as a religious Pharisee (3:4–7). One person described him as belonging to almost every kind of aristocracy that would excite the dreams and kindle the aspirations of men. Paul had been brought up as a Roman citizen. Nothing could be more humiliating for a man with his background than to be misunderstood, persecuted, and even imprisoned. Yet Paul had learned to be content in all his tribulations.

> *Paul knew ... that wherever he was, or in whatever circumstance he found himself, he was there by divine appointment. If he was hungry, it was because God wanted him to be hungry. If he was full, it was because his Lord had so planned it. Busily and faithfully engaged in the service of his King, he could say, "Even so, Father, for so it seemed good in Your sight."*[1]

1. Read Philippians 4:11 and look for three key words.

2. What do the three words "I have learned" tell you about contentment?

3. What is your definition of contentment?

"Contentment isn't getting what we want but being satisfied with what we have."[2]

4. What do you think Paul meant when he said, "I know . . . how to be abased" (Philippians 4:12)?

> *It is a blessed secret when the believer learns how to carry a high head with an empty stomach, an upright look with an empty pocket, a happy heart with an unpaid salary, joy in God when men are faithless.*[3]

5. What did Paul mean when he said, "I know how to abound" (Philippians 4:12)?

6. Paul wrote, "I have learned . . . I know . . . I know . . . I can."

In Philippians 4:13 he made another bold statement, "I can do all things." Were these self-righteous statements? Explain.

The Source of Contentment

7. What enables us to be content at all times and in all circumstances (Philippians 4:11–13)?

The Gk. for strengthen means, "to put power in." Because believers are in Christ (Gal. 2:20), He infuses them with His strength to sustain them until they receive some provision (Eph. 3:16–20; 2 Cor. 12:10).[4]

---

8. Paraphrase Philippians 4:13 in your own words.

My paraphrase is this: I can do all the things Christ asks me to do because He constantly infuses His power into me.

9. How do we get strength, or power, from God (Isaiah 40:31)?

Contentment is having that spiritual artesian well within so that you don't have to run to the broken cisterns of the world to get what you need. The power of Christ in the inner man is all we need for

> *the demands of life. Resources on the outside, such as friends and counselors and encouragements, are only helpful as they strengthen our resources on the inside.*[5]

10. As we spend time in God's Word, He infuses new strength in us for the challenges we will face. What do the following verses from Psalm 119 tell us God's Word will do for us?

Verse 11

Verses 49–52

Verses 65–67

Verse 105

Verse 130

Verses 161–164

11. Is contentment a struggle for you? Is reading God's Word a constant struggle? How are these two struggles related to each other?

Second Corinthians 11:23–28 describes the hardships Paul endured before he wrote to the believers in Philippi. He had learned to be content in whatever situation God put him in.

I once read of a missionary who worked with pygmies in Africa for fifty-two years. The conditions she lived in were unbearable. Sometimes she had to bring the thermometer inside for fear it would break in the scorching heat (120 degrees or higher). Yet she had learned to be content in her circumstances. How did she do it? Here is her prescription for contentment:

> *1. Allow thyself to complain of nothing, not even of the weather. 2. Never picture thyself to thyself under any circumstance in which thou art not. 3. Never compare thine own lot with that of another. 4. Never allow thyself to dwell on the wish that this or that had been, or were, otherwise than it was, or is. God Almighty loves thee better and more wisely than thou dost thyself. 5. Never dwell on the morrow. Remember that it is God's, not thine. The heaviest part of sorrow often is to look forward to it. "The Lord will provide."* [6]

Learning Contentment

12. How could Romans 8:28 and 29 help us not to complain about anything?

13. Which are you the most concerned about: being comfortable or being conformed to Christ? Why?

14. Are you wishing you could live somewhere else or be in a different circumstance? Explain.

15. How can Philippians 3:13 help us if we are wishing certain circumstances had never happened?

16. According to Matthew 6:34, what should we do if we wish to know about tomorrow?

17. Why do we need to keep focused on today and not worry about tomorrow?

Read again the missionary's prescription for contentment (p. 31). Mark the parts that apply to yesterday, those that cover today, and those that include tomorrow. If we are going to be content, we, too, must learn to follow this prescription. Most of us find that struggling with tomorrow gives us the most cause for discontentment. However, we must remember that all of our tomorrows are in God's hand and that He is already there. All we need to be concerned about is today.

18. Which one of the five points on the prescription for contentment are you struggling the most with right now? Explain.

"Every person lives in one of two tents: conTENT or disconTENT. In which do you live?"[7]

19. If you have never even tried to be content, what would you say is the first thing you need to do?

Learning to be content has been a gradual process in my life, but palms-up living has helped me in the process. I say, "Give what You want and take what You want." I can relate to Paul when he said, "I know both how to be abased, and I know how to abound" (Philippians 4:12).

 *From My Heart*

God wants to transform our lives. He wants us to learn to be content. Most of the world is unhappy and discontented, but He wants His children to be different—transformed. "And be not conformed to this world: but be ye transformed by the renewing of your mind, that ye may prove what is that good, and acceptable, and perfect, will of God" (Romans 12:2).

How are we transformed from discontented to contented women? Through the "renewing of your mind." We must renew, or refill, our minds with the Word of God each day to have the spiritual strength to be content no matter what is happening in our lives. As we immerse ourselves in the Word, the Holy Spirit strengthens our "inner man" (Ephesians 3:16). The Spirit's power through the Word could be compared to dipping a tea bag into hot water. The longer the tea bag stays in the water, the stronger it becomes. The more time we spend in the Word, the more strength is infused into us by the Holy Spirit, Who lives in us.

Vance Havner once said, "Lord, You've got the strength and I've got the weakness—let's team up." Pretty good advice!

From Your Heart

Have you tried to be content but constantly fail? Could it be that you have been trying to do it in your own strength? Make a commitment to God to read your Bible daily for the next thirty days. I guarantee you this: you will not be sorry, and you will be strengthened!

Notes

1. William MacDonald, *Believer's Bible Commentary,* ed. Art Farstad (Nashville: Thomas Nelson Publishers, 1989), 1980.

2. *God's Little Devotional Book for Women* (Tulsa: Honor Books, Inc., 1996), 168.

3. Selected quote in *Believer's Bible Commentary,* 1980.

4. John MacArthur, *The MacArthur Study Bible* (Nashville: Word Publishing, 1997), 1828.

5. Warren W. Wiersbe, *The Bumps Are What You Climb On* (Grand Rapids: Baker Book House, 1980), 132.

6. E. B. Pusey, quoted in *Daily Strength for Daily Needs,* comp. Mary W. Tileston (Uhrichsville, OH: Barbour and Company, Inc., 1990), 109, 110.

7. Benjamin R. De Jong, *Uncle Ben's Quotebook* (Irvine, CA: Harvest House Publishers, 1976), 116.

Learning to Be Content in Every Circumstance

"I know both how to be abased, and I know how to abound: every where and in all things I am instructed both to be full and to be hungry, both to abound and to suffer need" (Philippians 4:12).

E ven people who don't believe in God or profess to be born-again Christians are recognizing that an attitude of gratitude is a powerful source of health and well-being.

"*Mind and Body* . . . published an article entitled, 'Twenty Ways to Feel Calm, Happier, and Healthier,' and the number one answer was 'to be thankful for all the good in your life.' "[1]

A Grateful Attitude

The apostle Paul found that a God-centered, faith-oriented, thankful life worked for him, but he was not thankful only for the good in his life. In Philippians 4:11 he said he had learned to be content in every situation he found himself in: "Not that I speak in respect of want: for I have learned, in whatsoever state I am, therewith to be content."

First Thessalonians 5:18 and Ephesians 5:20 provide insight into how Paul learned to be content.

1. What does "in every thing give thanks" mean (1 Thessalonians 5:18)?

2. What does "for this is the will of God in Christ Jesus concerning you" mean (1 Thessalonians 5:18)?

> *More than 250 years ago, [Matthew Henry]*
> *wrote these words in his diary after he was robbed*
> *of all the money he had in the world. "Let me be*
> *thankful first, because I was never robbed before;*
> *second, because although they took my purse, they*
> *did not take my life; third, let me be thankful that*
> *although they took my all, it was not much; and*
> *fourth, because it was I who was robbed and not I*
> *who robbed." No doubt about it; thankfulness is a*
> *choice.* [2]

3. A professing believer once told my husband that he was
   thankful for the affair he was having because he felt it was
   God's will for him to be happy. How was his view of God dis-
   torted (Exodus 20:14)?

   It is never right to violate God's commands.

4. Ephesians 5:20 says, "Giving thanks always for all things unto
   God and the Father in the name of our Lord Jesus Christ."
   What two words in this verse are hard to accept and believe?
   Why?

A spirit of gratitude, instead of complaining, is a necessary
ingredient in learning contentment. Being grateful is a choice we
make. We choose our attitude of gratitude inwardly the same way
we choose the dress we will wear outwardly.

> *There is a legend of a man who found the barn where*
> *Satan kept his seeds ready to be sown in the human*
> *heart, and on finding the seeds of discouragement*
> *more numerous than others, learned that those seeds*
> *could be made to grow almost anywhere. When Satan*

> *was questioned he reluctantly admitted that there*
> *was one place in which he could never get them to*
> *thrive. "And where is that?" asked the man. Satan*
> *replied sadly, "In the heart of a grateful man."* [3]

5. Read Psalm 107. In this psalm, how many times does God say, "Oh that men would praise the LORD"? What does He want us to be grateful for?

If you ever read the book *Robinson Crusoe*, you know that the main character was shipwrecked and lived alone on a tropical island for twenty-eight years. How did he survive? Robinson Crusoe kept a journal of the comforts he enjoyed and the miseries he suffered. He made a deliberate choice to find things to be thankful for based on the reality he was facing.

6. Are you in a miserable situation with no known hope of escape? Maybe you should do as Robinson Crusoe did. List your complaints and your thanks below.

Complaints　　　　　　　　**Thanks**

If you are walking close to God, even though you may be in the midst of a dreadful situation, your thanks list will no doubt be longer than your complaint list. If you had a hard time finding things to be thankful for, name a characteristic of God for each letter of the alphabet. If that doesn't give you something to be thankful for, you need to question your relationship with God.

An ungrateful, complaining attitude left unchecked is certain to lead us into the wilderness of discontent, just as it did the Children of Israel.

7. Read Numbers 11:1. How did God feel when the Israelites complained? How does God feel about our complaining?

8. Read verses 14 and 15 of Numbers 11. How did the Israelites' complaining affect Moses? How does our complaining affect others?

A negative, ungrateful attitude can be changed to a positive, grateful, contented attitude. How does it happen? It happens when we, by an act of our wills, choose to think on Biblical things instead of sinful things. If we are ever going to learn to be content in every situation, we must learn to think right.

Sinful Thought Patterns

9. If we think sinful thoughts, how will they affect us (Proverbs 23:7)? If we think godly thoughts, how will they affect us (Philippians 4:8, 9)?

10. How can we learn to stop unbiblical and sinful thinking, according to 2 Corinthians 10:5?

11. What does it mean to take into captivity every thought (2 Corinthians 10:5)?

12. Why should we take captive our unbiblical and sinful thoughts?

How are strongholds destroyed? Patterns of negative thinking and behavior are learned, and they can be unlearned through disciplined Bible study and counseling.[4]

---

13. Philippians 4:8 gives us a list of things to think on if we want to live a worry-free, peaceful life. What is the first thing we should think on?

14. The word "true" in Philippians 4:8 could mean "real." Why would worrying about tomorrow be wrong, according to this verse?

15. How might thinking "if-only thoughts" about a past circumstance be considered thinking on something untrue, or unreal?

> *We need to remember that the future is not real.*
> *The future exists only in our imagination. . . .*
> *And the past is no more real than the future. . . .*
> *"If only I had done that differently." . . . Such "if*
> *only" thinking is counterproductive, first, because*
> *it doesn't address what is real. The past is gone. It*
> *is beyond repair or restructuring. What is real is*
> *what is happening today, and God calls us to deal*
> *with what is now.*[5]

If you are fearful, unhappy, and discontented in your circumstances, you can be sure you have been dwelling on Satan's lies. God tells us to "put on the whole armour of God, that ye may be able to stand against the wiles of the devil" (Ephesians 6:11). One of our pieces of armor is the Word of God (v. 17).

16. Listed below are some principles and promises from God's Word. Replace your unbiblical thoughts with these truths. Look up each verse and write the principle or promise.

Psalm 103:13 and 14 and 1 John 1:7–9

Psalm 130:1–8

Isaiah 40:11

1 Samuel 16:7

Jeremiah 31:3

Psalm 91:14–16

1 Peter 5:7

Daily Mental Exercise

Here is a mental exercise for you to learn to think on Biblical principles and promises. Each day this week think on a truth from God's Word when you find yourself thinking unbiblical thoughts.

Sunday—God is my protector.

> *"He that dwelleth in the secret place of the most High shall abide under the shadow of the Almighty. I will say of the* Lord, *He is my refuge and my fortress: my God; in him will I trust"* *(Psalm 91:1, 2).*

Monday—God always does what is right!

> *"Shall not the Judge of all the earth do right?"* *(Genesis 18:25).*

Tuesday—God hears me and wants to help me.

> *"I sought the* Lord, *and he heard me, and delivered me from all my fears" (Psalm 34:4).*

Wednesday—God is near me.

> *"Whither shall I go from thy spirit? or whither shall I flee from thy presence?" (Psalm 139:7).*

Thursday—God has good things planned for His people, including me.

> *"For I know the thoughts that I think toward you, saith the* Lord, *thoughts of peace, and not of evil, to give you an expected end" (Jeremiah 29:11).*

Friday—God will not give up on me.

> *"Being confident of this very thing, that he which hath begun a good work in you will perform it until the day of Jesus Christ" (Philippians 1:6).*

Saturday—God will never give me more than I can bear.

> *"But God is faithful, who will not suffer you to be [tested] above that ye are able; but will with the [testing] also make a way to escape, that ye may be able to bear it" (1 Corinthians 10:13).*

Don't forget, "For as he thinketh in his heart, so is he" (Proverbs 23:7). You can't be discouraged unless you are thinking discouraging thoughts. Biblical thoughts lead to an attitude of gratitude, and an attitude of gratitude leads you to contentment. Only you can make those choices—will you?

 ## *From My Heart*

Having been a pastor's wife for over forty years and dealing with hundreds of women, I have come to this conclusion: many women have never enjoyed a contented life because their emotions are controlled by their circumstances. Focusing on their circumstances, instead of on the God of their circumstances, puts them on a roller coaster that is unrelated to true contentment. Their contentment depends upon how people treat them, how much money or how many things they have, and the list goes on and on. They find no contentment in God and how He works in their lives. It is as if they forgot God is in control of what they have or don't have. As a result, they also forget He is working all things together for their spiritual good (Romans 8:28, 29).

The secret of contentment? An understanding of God's sovereign control keeps everything in perspective. Failure to understand this truth robs us of contentment.

Palms-up living has helped me learn to be content and to say, "Whatever, Lord!"

From Your Heart

Are you discontent and discouraged? Have you been dwelling on unbiblical thoughts most of the time? How do you need to change your thinking? Did you try the seven-day exercise (p. 41)? If not, will you start today?

Notes

1. James MacDonald, *Lord, Change My Attitude* (Chicago: Moody Press, 2001), 50.

2. Ibid., 61.

3. Cowman, 250.

4. Neil T. Anderson, *The Bondage Breaker* (Eugene, OR: Harvest House Publishers, 1993), 152–154.

5. Elizabeth George, *Loving God with All Your Mind* (Eugene, OR: Harvest House Publishers, 1994), 36, 38.

Learning to Be Content in Your Relationships

"And when ye stand praying, forgive, if you have ought against any: that your Father also which is in heaven may forgive you your trespasses"
(Mark 11:25).

Learning to be content with all the people my life touches seems to be an utter impossibility sometimes. We all can relate to these words: "To dwell above with those we love, oh, that will be glory, / To dwell below with those we know, well—that's another story!"

Good relationships bring us untold joy and a great sense of contentment. However, if we have an unforgiving, bitter spirit, we need only one broken relationship to affect all our relationships. As Scripture warns, "Lest any root of bitterness springing up trouble you, and thereby many be defiled" (Hebrews 12:15).

Broken Relationships

Have you been offended or deeply hurt by someone? If so, do any of the statements below relate to you?

- I still feel angry every time I think of how _____ treated me.
- Deep in my heart I have a secret desire that _____ pays for what he (or she) did to me.
- If I do not watch myself, I find myself telling others how much

  _____ hurt me.

These statements indicate that we have not fully forgiven the person who hurt us.

We don't think of ourselves as "unforgiving" or "bitter"—those words imply that we are somehow personally responsible. We prefer to talk about how deeply we have been "hurt," implying that we are merely helpless victims. Are those who have been deeply wounded destined to live damaged lives? Or is there real healing for deep hurt? I say there is. ... We've also deceived ourselves into believing that we can love and serve God and be "good Christians," while failing to forgive. When are we going to get honest? [1]

Let's look at some of the reasons people use for holding on to an unforgiving spirit.

The number one reason of most people is that they've been *hurt too deeply*.

1. Who suffered more than we can even comprehend, and why did He suffer (Isaiah 53:3–7)?

2. Christ loved us enough to die for us. Yet we keep hurting and grieving Him with our sin. How does He treat us (Jeremiah 31:34; Isaiah 43:25; Ephesians 4:32; 1 John 1:9)?

When our God forgives us, He promises that He will not remember our sins against us anymore. ... To "not remember" is simply a graphic way of saying, "I will not bring up these matters to you or others in the future. I will bury them and not exhume the bones to beat you over the head with them. I will never use these sins against you." [2]

3. How do we exhume dead bones and beat people over the head with them?

4. When we hurt Christ, He forgives us. How did Christ tell us to treat those who hurt us (Luke 6:27)?

5. Read Philippians 2:13 and 4:13. Christ did not tell us to forgive or love our enemies without helping us do it. How does He help us?

6. Do you need to forgive someone who has offended you before your lack of forgiveness hurts or even breaks your relationship with that person? If you answered yes, will you right now confess your sin of harboring an unforgiving spirit (1 John 1:9)?

Another reason people hold on to an unforgiving spirit is that they *don't think the offenders deserve forgiveness*. They need to pay for what they did!

7. Do you deserve God's forgiveness? What have you done to earn it (Ephesians 2:8, 9)?

8. What does God say about making people pay or trying to get even (Romans 12:17–21)?

> *Remember: Letting the offender off of your hook does not mean they are off of God's hook. Forgiveness involves transferring the prisoner over to the One who is able and responsible to mete out justice. It relieves us of the burden and responsibility to hold them in prison ourselves.*[3]

9. Broken relationships make life miserable and rob us of contentment. How do most people deal with broken relationships?

When a relationship is broken, most people attack the person rather than the problem. Another mistake people make in broken relationships is to ignore or cover them up, as if they had not happened. Words inflicted in the heart must be dealt with, or they will grow like a cancer. Some people treat relationships as disposable goods; they just discard them. Fixing relationships seems to be more trouble than the relationships are worth.

10. How does God picture, or illustrate, trying to win back the friendship of an offended person (Proverbs 18:19)?

Broken relationships can be made worse if we handle them in the wrong way. Let's look at God's way of healing a broken relationship.

Restoring a Broken Relationship

God sent His Son, Jesus Christ, to the earth to repair the relationship between God and us that was broken by sin. "God was in Christ, reconciling the world unto himself" (2 Corinthians 5:19).

11. Read 1 John 4:9 and 10. What was the first step God took so that we can have peace with Him?

12. Read Jeremiah 31:3. What kind of love must we have in our hearts before we can work toward restoring a relationship?

13. What three words do you see in Philippians 2:8 that are necessary to restore broken human relationships? (Hint: They are what Christ did.)

14. What is one of the biggest hindrances in settling human disputes or broken relationships? (Hint: It's the opposite of what is found in Ephesians 4:1–3.)

15. What did Christ, the One Who did no wrong, endure so that we can have peace with God? What might we have to endure to heal a broken human relationship (1 Peter 3:18; 4:1)?

16. Can you recall an incident in which you were willing to suffer to restore a relationship? What was it?

The New Testament speaks of a covering forgiveness as well as one that confronts. . . . When Jesus describes covering forgiveness in Mark 11:25, there is no mention of confronting the individual who needs to be forgiven. This is confirmed in 1 Peter 4:8 which tells us that "love covers a multitude of sins." If the only method for expressing forgiveness involved confronting the individual who hurt us, no matter how large or small the hurt, we would spend our time doing little else. . . . How can we know when to employ those two distinctly different methods? Very simply. Covering forgiveness should always be viewed as the first option. If the "cover" doesn't stay on, but keeps flying off, no matter how many times you may put it back on, then you must use option two—confronting forgiveness.[4]

17. What did Christ tell believers to do when conflicts exist (Matthew 18:15)?

A face-to-face encounter with the other person may not resolve the problem. According to Matthew 18:16, if private confrontation fails, we should enlist the help of others. The wisdom and influence outsiders may bring can be helpful. And even if the problem remains, they can still be witnesses to guard against any misrepresentation of the things discussed.[5]

18. We deserve to be punished because of our sin, but God is gracious and forgives us (Ephesians 1:7). What is Christ's command to us in Ephesians 4:32 and Luke 17:4?

Augustine wrote, "If you are suffering from a bad man's injustice, forgive him lest there be two bad men." [6]

As we view the life of Jesus Christ, we see the steps that God took to repair broken relationships. These are the same steps we must take.

- He loved us. We must love the person unconditionally.
- He humbled Himself for us. We must put aside our pride and hurt feelings and must humble ourselves.
- He suffered for us. We must be willing to suffer more hurt and pain.
- He invited us to be reconciled to Him. We must we willing to take the first step in reconciliation.
- He forgave us. We must forgive whether the offender asks for forgiveness or not.

Are you haunted by a broken relationship that you know you should try to mend? You will never know contentment until you make an effort at reconciliation.

 *From My Heart*

Finding contentment in my relationships is not something that just happens; it is something I will have to work on the rest of my life. I am not perfect, and neither are my brothers and sisters in Christ. We are all forgiven sinners who wear the placard, "Be patient. I'm not perfect yet." Because I'm not perfect, I may hurt and sometimes deeply wound another person. Our friends in the world are even worse because they don't have the Holy Spirit in them to help curb sin. Therefore, I can expect disappointment and hurts in my relationships.

Christ knew we would suffer the pains and hurts He experienced, yet He commanded us to forgive. Remember, a command is not something we do if we feel like it. All our broken relationships do not need to be restored, but they all need to have "forgiven" written over them. We don't forgive someone just for that person's sake but also for our sake so we can be free from an unforgiving, bitter spirit. I have learned that forgiveness is costly. I may live with the consequences of another person's sin for the rest of my life. However, I have also learned that I will live with the consequences no matter what I do. The big question I have to ask myself is, Will I live with the consequences in freedom or imprisoned with an unforgiving, bitter spirit? To forgive is to set a prisoner free and to discover that the prisoner was me.

The choice is ours: to forgive or not to forgive! The first results in contentment; the other, in discontent.

Contentment in my relationships also involves palms-up living. Telling the Lord to give or take a relationship can be really hard, but it keeps me free to enjoy the contented life!

From Your Heart

In your personal history, is there a broken relationship that you know should be restored? What are you going to do about it? When are you going to do it?

Notes

1. Byron Paulus, "From the Executive Director," *Spirit of Revival* (August 1993), 2.

2. Jay Adams, *From Forgiven to Forgiving* (Amityville, NY: Calvary Press, 1994), 12.

3. "Making It Personal," *Spirit of Revival* (August 1993), 32.

4. Henry Igras, *Why Me?* (Ozark, AL: ACW Press: 2005), 168, 169.

5. James Pittman, *What to Do with a Broken Relationship* (Grand Rapids: Radio Bible Class, 1987), 17.

6. Augustine, quoted in *What to Do with a Broken Relationship* (Grand Rapids: Radio Bible Class, 1987), 26.

Learning to Be Content without Worrying

"Take therefore no thought for the morrow: for the morrow shall take thought for the things of itself. Sufficient unto the day is the evil thereof"
(Matthew 6:34).

You can never learn to be content until you learn to handle your worries instead of letting them handle you. Some experts name "worry" as public enemy number one.

Worry is not a sideline issue; it is a major problem in our society, and no one is free from the ravages of its poison. It affects our total being. . . . We have become a computer driven society with the ability to unleash information into offices and homes in a matter of seconds. We have imaging machines that can peer into the body with precision. Our accomplishments are miraculous, but we have not yet learned how to handle the basic mental power within us. Worry is still waiting to be conquered.[1]

1. How do you define worry?

2. The word "worry" comes from the Greek word *mirimnos,* which is a combination of two words, *merizo* ("to divide") and *nous* ("mind"). How does James 1:8 describe a divided mind?

3. What do young women worry about? older women? all women?

4. One writer calls worry the "God can't" disease. When we say, "God can't," what are we calling God (Luke 1:37; 1 John 5:10)?

5. How can we compare worry to a disease? How is it different from a real disease?

6. How ridiculous is worry in God's sight (Matthew 6:27)?

Worry is not something someone else forces upon us. It is something that we choose to do ourselves.[2]

Six Reasons Why Worry Is Ridiculous
(1) It is unreasonable.
(2) It is unnecessary.
(3) It is unwise.
(4) It is unhealthy.
(5) It is unproductive.
(6) It is sin.

Biblical Solutions

Let's look at some Biblical solutions for these six reasons.

7. Worry is unreasonable (Matthew 6:34). Why is worrying about tomorrow unreasonable?

8. How can we plan for tomorrow without worrying about tomorrow?

9. Worry is unnecessary (Philippians 4:19). Why does God tell us worry is unnecessary?

10. Are you worrying about any of these needs: physical needs, financial needs, spiritual needs? Why?

Needs	What You're Worried About	Why You're Worried
Physical		
Financial		
Spiritual		

11. How concerned do you think God is about these needs (Matthew 10:29–31; 1 Peter 5:7)?

12. Worry is unwise (Isaiah 40:28, 29; 41:10, 13). Why is worry unwise?

13. Worry is unhealthy (Psalm 42:5, 11). Worry makes us feel downhearted and discouraged emotionally. How can worry affect us physically?

14. Worry is unproductive (Philippians 3:13). Someone has said that worrying about our past failures is as unproductive as sawing sawdust. Why is this observation true?

> *Freedom from worry can never be accomplished if we insist on dragging the past around with us. Much of our worry is "stuff" left over from yesterday, like garbage we pull along, refusing to let go, until we can't move. Paul gave us good advice when he said, "This thing I do: forgetting what lies behind . . . I press on" (Philippians 3:13, 14). The past is past—leave it alone.*[3]

15. Worry is sin (Philippians 4:6, 7; James 4:17). Why is it sinful to worry?

> *What harm does [worry] do? If it doesn't do any good,*
> *does it do any harm? That puts it in quite a different*
> *light. "Worry," said William A. Ward, "distorts our*
> *thinking, disrupts our work, disquiets our soul,*
> *disturbs our body, disfigures our face, destroys*
> *our poise, depresses our friends, demoralizes our*
> *life, defeats our faith, and debilitates our energy."*
> *If worry doesn't do us any good, it sure does us a*
> *lot of harm!* [4]

Would you agree that worry is not only sinful but ridiculous?

Overcoming Worrying

Let's consider how Philippians 4 can help us overcome worry.

16. What steps do you see in Philippians 4:4–9 for overcoming worry?

Verse 4

Verse 5

Verse 6

Verse 7

Verses 8 and 9

Verse 10

> *The biggest problem you and I have to deal with*
> *. . . is choosing the right thoughts. . . . The great*
> *philosopher of the Roman Empire, Marcus Aurelius,*
> *summed it up in eight words . . . : "Our life is what*
> *our thoughts make it." . . . Yes, if we think happy*
> *thoughts, we will be happy. If we think miserable*
> *thoughts, we will be miserable.* [5]

17. What actions did Paul take that we can take to overcome worry (Philippians 4:11, 12)? How would you translate the truth in verse 13 into a step you can take to overcome worry?

    Verses 11 and 12

    Verse 13

18. How would you translate the truths in Philippians 4:19 into steps you can take for overcoming worry?

> *Contentment comes from adequate resources. Our*
> *resources are the providence of God, the power of*
> *God, and the promises of God. These resources made*
> *Paul sufficient for every demand of life, and they*
> *can make us sufficient, too.* [6]

When we use the resources God has available for us, we can trust God with yesterday, today, and tomorrow and enjoy a life of contentment.

 **From My Heart**

How do I live without worrying? I don't! However, I do worry less and less as I get to know God better and better. Getting to know God better each day is a top priority to keep me in the path of obedience. When I make my "Things to Do" list each day, I put "Time with the Lord" as the first thing on my list because He has told me, "Seek ye first the kingdom of God, and his righteousness" (Matthew 6:33). When I fully understand His importance in my life, it is easier to give Him the proper place of priority. With His help and strength (Philippians 4:13), I can worry less and trust Him more. When I don't draw upon His help, I find myself worrying and trying to fix things that only He can fix. Christ reminds me, "For without me ye can do nothing" (John 15:5).

Let me give you a few practical tips to help break the worry habit.

- Put a rubber band on your wrist. Every time you start worrying, snap yourself and say, "I am not trusting God—this thing I'm worrying about is sin."
- Instead of worrying, start working on your problem. Write down and answer these questions: What is my problem? What does God want me to do about it? When, where, and how should I begin?
- Turn every care into a prayer. What have you been worrying about? Start praying about it.

A famous preacher was asked if he worried. "Oh, of course not," he answered, "because worry is sin, and if I'm going to sin, I would choose something that's a lot more fun."

Do you do drugs? get drunk? commit adultery? worry? Sin is sin in God's eyes, and I think He finds worrying just as disgusting as the other sins I have mentioned.

I am making a new commitment to God to worry less and trust Him more. Will you? Remember that contentment comes from our confident trust in God and our relationship with Him, not from circumstances or people. Again I must say, with palms up, "Give what You want and take what You want."

From Your Heart

Do you have a hard time viewing worry as sin? Why? What do you worry about the most? What one thing in this lesson could help you overcome worry?

Notes

1. Robert H. Spain, *How to Stay Alive as Long as You Live* (Nashville: Dimensions For Living, 1992), 60, 61.

2. Richard Lee, *The Unfailing Promise* (Waco, Texas: Word Books, 1988), 91.

3. Spain, 64.

4. Donald W. Morgan, *How to Get It Together When Your World Is Coming Apart* (Grand Rapids: Fleming H. Revell, 1988), 89.

5. Dale Carnegie, *How to Stop Worrying and Start Living* (New York: Simon and Schuster, 1948), 89.

6. Warren W. Wiersbe, *Be Joyful* (Wheaton, IL: Victor Books, 1974), 127.

Learning to Be Content with Who You Are

"Man looketh on the outward appearance, but the
LORD looketh on the heart" (1 Samuel 16:7).

N one of us can ever learn to be content with where we are and where we are going in life until we're content with who we are. What mental picture do you have of yourself? Do you like the picture you see?

I always have one thing I can be thankful for, even on a bad-hair day. I am thankful I don't look as bad as the picture of myself that I carry around in my wallet—my driver's license picture. I am always a little embarrassed to show it as a form of identification. Yet I am also thankful, telling myself, "I don't really look that bad."

This picture I carry of myself may not be a good picture, but it is real. The mental picture we carry around with us, the one no one else sees, may not be a good picture, but it is real to us.

> *Research has shown that we tend to act in harmony with our mental self-portrait. If we don't like the kind of person we are, we think no one else likes us either. And that influences our social life, our job performance, our relationships with others.*[1]

1. What is the word psychologists have given for the mental picture we have of ourselves?

61

2. What are other words used for self-image?

Whether we label it "self-image," "self-esteem," or "self-worth," the need to feel loved, accepted, and successful in what we do is crucial to our emotional and spiritual well-being. I repeat the questions I started with, What mental picture do you have of yourself? Is it a Biblically accurate, realistic picture?

> *I am here to tell you that your self-portrait is not permanently affixed in place like a photo encased in plastic in your wallet. You can change it. You can develop a more accurate and healthy view of yourself. True, weaknesses, blind spots, and natural tendencies may occasionally distort the picture, but, as you learn to see yourself as God sees you, that distortion factor will decrease.*[2]

None of us are as emotionally and spiritually well-balanced as we would like to be. All of us should be able to repeat these words: "I'm not what I want to be. I'm not what I ought to be. But, praise God, I'm not what I used to be!"

We all had parents who weren't perfect, and we aren't perfect either. Therefore, we all have what the world calls "dysfunctional families." Before we came into a personal relationship with Jesus Christ, our thinking and actions were messed up, but when we were born-again, we were transformed.

3. How do we know and demonstrate that we have been transformed (2 Corinthians 5:17; Ephesians 4:17–29; Colossians 3:5–10)?

At His friend's graveside, Jesus said, "Lazarus, come forth" (John 11:43). Upon Jesus' command a dead person became alive. Then He said, "Loose him, and let him go."

4. Why do the "graveclothes" people wore before they were born again often keep them bound (Ephesians 4:22–24)?

God transforms us and makes us new creations when we are born again. Romans 12:2 tells us not to be conformed to this world, or not to let the world squeeze us into its mold.

5. How will constantly wanting acceptance from the world affect how we feel about ourselves and our outward beauty?

6. Does God emphasize outward or inward beauty (1 Samuel 16:7)?

7. How does God view outward beauty (Proverbs 31:30; 1 Peter 3:3, 4)? What does this imply about a woman who is more concerned with outward beauty than with inner beauty?

Whether I'm clipping coupons, reading the paper, or searching for information online, I am bombarded by advertisements carrying the elusive promise of a thinner, newer, better me. . . . Hair products promise to give more bounce to curls or remove unwanted curl. Skin products promise blemish-free skin when we're young and wrinkle-free skin when we're old. We are obsessed with self-dissatisfaction. . . .

Desiring acceptance from the world, we undertake any number of measures to look like the world says we should look. From endless diets to radical and cosmetic surgeries, creams to pills, clothes to shoes, we keep trying to recreate ourselves in the world's image of perfection.[3]

8. Read 1 Corinthians 13:11. In what way have you had a "childish," or immature, understanding of beauty?

Transformed, Not Conformed

Don't be conformed to the world—be transformed by God.

9. When we are transformed by God, what should radiate from our lives (Psalm 90:17)?

10. How can needing beautiful clothes and the "right" makeup and hairstyle to feel beautiful or valuable be idolatry (Exodus 20:2–4)?

A carving of stone or gold is not an idol in and of itself. The heart of the worshiper is what makes an object an idol. Jewelry, makeup, and clothing do not have the power to be idols in and of themselves. The motive of my heart (what I desire from those things) determines whether or not they are idols. If I need jewelry, makeup, or fashionable clothing to feel valuable, I have transformed those objects into idols because I expect from them what I can receive only from the One I claim to worship.[4]

Seeing Ourselves as God Sees Us

As we mature in our love for God and begin to see ourselves as He sees us, all of our yearnings for love and acceptance begin to be filled.

11. What should we see ourselves as having (Jeremiah 31:3)?

12. How is God's kind of love different from other people's love?

13. What does God call us so that we see ourselves as accepted by Him (John 15:13–15)?

14. When we see ourselves as God sees us, we see ourselves as valuable and significant. What can we do because we have the Holy Spirit in us (Philippians 4:13)?

15. Why should "I can't change" no longer be part of a born-again believer's vocabulary (Galatians 2:20)?

16. What should we view ourselves as having for making the right choices (James 1:5)?

17. What have we been delivered from, and what has happened to all our sins? This is how we view ourselves as we mature in Christ (1 John 1:6, 7; Ephesians 1:7).

When we see ourselves as God sees us, we see ourselves as people of great value and worth—no more and no less.

18. Our past, which was filled with fear and guilt, no longer has to haunt us. What should characterize our re-created life (2 Timothy 1:7)?

19. Why isn't our new life always filled with love, power, and a sound mind (Galatians 5:16–23), and whose fault is that (Romans 8:5, 6)?

Can a weak-willed human being actually experience love, forgiveness and a practical victory over sin? Yes, by meditating upon the Word. Here's how it works. Are you having a problem with sensual lust? Memorize and personalize Romans 6—8. Live with these three chapters day and night. Meditate upon the principles found in them while eating, working, daydreaming, showering, walking and driving. Meanwhile, ask the Holy Spirit to pump reality and joy into what you are pondering. Watch what happens after one year. You'll be amazed at the transformation that will have taken place. A renewed mind. "But what if I get blown off course?" you may ask. . . . The Emergency Room of the Bible is 1 John 1:9, "If we confess our sins, He is faithful and just to forgive us our sins and to cleanse us from all unrighteousness." What seems to be so simple is actually profound. What seems to be so profound is actually simple.[5]

20. How can we know if we are growing spiritually and in our Biblically based view of ourselves (Colossians 2:8; 1 Corinthians 2:16)?

Palms-up living has helped me so much in learning to be content with who I am and what God wants me to be.

 *From My Heart*

I am amazed that God knows me inside and out and still loves me. Every time I read Psalm 139, I am reminded how well God knows yet loves me. He never lets me out of His sight. Yes, the One Who knows me the best loves me the most. God not only loves me unconditionally—when I am good and when I am bad—but He accepts me unconditionally just the way I am. I do not have to earn His love by my performance; therefore, I know I cannot lose His love (Ephesians 2:8, 9; Romans 8:38, 39). My acceptance is based on Who He is and what He has done for me, not what I do for Him.

I am Christ's workmanship (Ephesians 2:10), and He expects the best from me. He wants me to succeed and have a sense of significance; however, when I fail as I so often do, He forgives me and wants me to try again (1 John 1:9). I have learned in my walk with God that I am not a failure if I fall, but I am a failure if I don't get up and try again. I have also learned that nothing is too hard for the Lord (Genesis 18:14). He specializes in the impossible (Luke 1:37). He is able to work my failures into His plans for me (Jeremiah 29:11). Because I am so valuable in His sight, He always has my best interests at heart. Oh, by the way, He feels the same way about you!

From Your Heart

Have the needs for love, acceptance, and significance been met in your life? Have you seen how these needs *can* be met in Christ? Which thought from this lesson helped you the most?

Notes

1. Josh McDowell, *Building Your Self-Image* (Wheaton, IL: Tyndale House Publishers, Inc., 1984), 20.

2. Ibid., 21.

3. Regina Franklin, *Who Calls Me Beautiful?* (Grand Rapids: Discovery House Publishers, 2004), 10, 11.

4. Ibid., 69.

5. Joel A. Freeman, *Living with Your Conscience Without Going Crazy* (San Bernardino, CA: Here's Life Publishers, Inc., 1989), 57.

Learning to Be Content with Just Enough

"If riches increase, set not your heart upon them"
(Psalm 62:10).

When I started writing this book, thoughts about contentment were always in the back of my mind. This thought caught my attention and stimulated my thinking to develop a lesson on "Just Enough": *The rich person is not the person who has the most, but the one who doesn't need more.*

I have learned, and am still learning, that a truly contented person can say, "I have enough; I am satisfied." If I focus on something that is bigger or better, I do not feel content. Enough is never enough.

Years ago my husband and I adopted a new style of living. We called it "living in your box." This lifestyle has allowed us to say, "Enough is enough."

Research shows that almost all people are dissatisfied with their incomes, whatever they are, and that they think all their troubles will be over when they get more money. Yet the more they get, the more they want. Enough is never enough.

1. What do you think "living in your box" means?

The Bible says a lot about money and possessions (over 1,000 references). Jesus talked more about money than He did about Heaven, Hell, and prayer. The Bible tells us about rich people, such as Job, Abraham, and Solomon.

> *We may begin to wonder why the Word of God talks so much about money, money matters, possessions, and materialism. Is it because money is the most important thing in scripture? No, I really think it's because God knew that we would have more problems trying to handle material possessions than any other area of living. He knew that it would be more difficult for us to believe, trust, and apply to our lives what the Word of God has to say concerning material possessions than any other area of scripture.*[1]

2. Proverbs 4:23 says, "Keep [guard] thy heart with all diligence; for out of it are the issues of life." Satan probably won't tempt us to rob a bank; however, he does tempt us constantly in three areas. What are they (1 John 2:16)?

3. What have you been allowing your eyes to dwell on that you know you can't afford but that you are determined to have anyway? Will that thing or stuff bring lasting peace or contentment to your heart? Explain.

God tells us that we will "always [have] all sufficiency in all things" and that we are "enriched in every thing to all bountifulness" (2 Corinthians 9:8–11). His Word also tells us to "love not the world, neither the things that are in the world" (1 John 2:15).

4. How can you discern whether you are *enjoying* the things God has given you or *loving* them?

God or Money?

Is God or money controlling your lifestyle? Many people serve their money whether they realize it or not. They are a slave to it and never feel free.

5. How we spend our money is an indicator of our hearts. What does it tell us (Luke 16:13)?

When we are in debt, we are money's servant rather than letting our money serve and bless us. When we learn to live in our box, we are no longer in bondage to our money. My husband and I arrived at a lifestyle that we thought we could maintain and enjoy for the rest of our lives. We determined that if our income increased beyond the point we had fixed for our lifestyle, we would save more and give away more.

6. Read Psalm 62:10. How does this verse illustrate the idea of living in your box?

I would challenge you to choose a lifestyle. Don't let your income dictate your lifestyle. Choose a comfortable level of living that you need, and do not compromise that with more spending when more income arrives. If you don't choose a lifestyle, this culture will choose one for you, and it will be the lifestyle of living beyond your means.[2]

7. What do companies constantly entice us with that allows us to live beyond our means and requires us to pay *them* for getting us into unmanageable debt?

If you pay off your credit card debt each month, you pay no interest. The card is a servant or service to you. However, if you pay that high interest each month and never pay off your debt, you are a servant to the credit card. You may need to perform "plastic surgery" on all your credit cards. Cut them up and throw them away!

In a book that was published in 1998, I learned that the typical American carries five to seven credit cards. In a magazine published in April 2005, I read the following:

> *People all around us are making mistakes in handling money. But financial blunders constitute one area in which we don't want to join the crowd. For example, the current personal savings rate approximates 1 percent annually; the average credit card balance is currently approaching $9,000; giving to ministries ranges between 2 to 2.5 percent of household income.*[3]

8. If we put loving and serving God ahead of serving our money, what does He promise to provide for us (Matthew 6:24–33)?

For God, Not Self

We're to use our money and possessions for God, not for selfish purposes.

9. Read Matthew 6:19–24. Are these verses telling us that if God blesses us with wealth, it is wrong to have a lovely home, bank accounts, and so forth? Explain.

10. How do Proverbs 30:8 and 9 picture being content with just enough?

On Loan

Everything we have is a loan to us from God.

11. Read Job 1:21. How did Job respond when God gave and then took away his riches? Why did he respond that way?

12. Do you need all of your things and stuff to be content? What did Jesus say about our things (Luke 12:15)?

13. Read Luke 12:15–21. What key phrase do you see in verse 21 that explains our discontent?

The Formula for Contentment

God's formula for contentment is
        Godliness + Contentment = Great Gain!

14. Contentment has a partner. What is it (1 Timothy 6:6)?

15. We arrived in this world naked and empty-handed. How will we leave (1 Timothy 6:7)?

16. God says that all we need for contentment is room and board. How is this truth illustrated in 1 Timothy 6:8?

> *I'm not saying a larger home or a second home is wrong. I'm just saying you don't have to have it, and the pursuit of it often leads to misery! You just need food and covering. That's enough. There's a Roman proverb, "Money is like seawater; once you drink, the thirstier you get." Well, contentment is breaking that cycle of thirst and being able to say, "I don't need anymore." "If we have food and covering, with these we shall be content" (1 Timothy 6:8). Content. That's saying: "I have enough."* [4]

17. What warning does God give to those who want to accumulate more and more material things and have bigger and bigger bank accounts (1 Timothy 6:9)?

18. Is God telling us to hate money in 1 Timothy 6:10? Explain.

19. Read 1 Timothy 6:10 again. How does the love of money lead people away from God, and what is their end?

If you want to be contented, you must come to the place where you can say, "I have enough." Then add to that, "Lord, it all belongs to You. Give what You want and take what You want."

 ## *From My Heart*

It took me a long time to learn that having just one more thing really didn't make me any happier. When I had this mentality, I never enjoyed what I had because I was always thinking about the next thing I wanted to get. I am learning to be content with what I have by not focusing on what I want and being grateful for what I have.

If we don't change our mind-set about always getting more, even if we get everything we want, we won't be content. Why? Because the same mind-set that wants more now will want more later. Here are a few tips for "living in your box":

- Choose contentment as a lifestyle. Strive to come to a place where you really believe you do not need to have more to be happier.
- Learn to think and say, "I have enough; I don't need more."
- Choose a comfortable level of living and do not compromise that lifestyle with more spending if you make more money.

My husband and I have been living in our box for many years now and are reaping the benefits of our contented lifestyle. Because we decided to save more and give more as God blessed us with more income, we are able to serve at our church for a minimum salary because we don't need more—we have enough. We also have enough to give to others who need our help.

"Godliness with contentment is great gain" (1 Timothy 6:6). I encourage you to try it.

From Your Heart

What did you learn about yourself as you studied this lesson? Are you content with your lifestyle, or do you think you need to change? What are you going to do about it?

Notes

1. Bruce Petersen, "Total Life Management" (Schroon Lake, NY, photocopy, n.d.), 85.

2. James MacDonald, 96.

3. Mark Robbins, "Financial Spring Cleaning," *The Baptist Bulletin* (April 2005), 22.

4. James MacDonald, 91.

Learning to Be Content regardless of the What-ifs

"What time I am afraid, I will trust in thee"
(Psalm 56:3).

W hat puts us in a prison of doubt? Most generally it is our fear of the future—the what-ifs. Have the what-ifs of life ever put you in a prison of doubt and fear? Are you in that prison right now?

In the allegory Pilgrim's Progress, *John Bunyan told of the soul's pilgrimage through this life. In one scene, two characters, Christian and Hopeful, were tired of traveling down the rough road and chose to journey across By-path Meadow instead. There they were captured by Giant Despair and thrown into Doubting Castle. For days they were held captive in Doubting Castle. Finally, Christian could stand no more and cried out, "What a fool am I, thus to lie in a stinking dungeon, when I may as well walk at liberty! I have a key in my bosom, called Promise, that will, I am persuaded, open any lock in Doubting Castle." Christian reached into his coat and pulled from it the key called Promise. He thrust it into the lock, gave it a turn, and opened the door. Thus Christian and his friend Hopeful were set free to travel again on the King's Highway. In our humanity it is easy to become imprisoned by fear and despair. But we need not remain there. Thrust in the key called Promise, and as you do, your fears will diminish; your despair, no matter*

how large a giant it seems to be, will flee; and your
faith will be set free.[1]

The key that unlocks the prison door of doubt is "Promise"—
the promises of God in His Word. Before we look at promises that
unlock the door of fear, let's look at the source of our fears.

The Source of Our Fears

1. Our fears do not come from God. Who, then, instigates our
   fears (2 Timothy 1:7; 1 Peter 5:8)?

Satan uses many sources to attack us. Four of these sources are
people, problems, possibilities, and perplexities.

People

2. Are people, or a person, causing you to fear? If so, what are
   you fearful of?

3. Read Psalm 56:4 and Hebrews 13:5. People may leave us,
   reject us, abandon us, or die. How do these verses quiet our
   fears?

Problems

4. What problem are you dealing with that is causing you to be
   fearful? How can Psalm 56:3 and Isaiah 26:3 help you?

5. How does a fear become a phobia? How can you get rid of this kind of fear (1 John 4:18)?

6. How does a perfect, or mature, love for God help us cast out fear (1 John 4:18)?

An eminent psychiatrist, Dr. Gerald G. Jampolsky, says the opposite of love is not hate. No, the opposite of love is fear. That means, to overcome fear, fill your life with love. Let love become the dominant force in your life. First John 4:18: "There is no fear in love; but perfect love casts out fear." . . . Love in your heart frees you from fear; relates you to the Source of Life, God; and releases positive feelings to overcome hostility, redress wrongs, heal hurts, and build relationships. Love is the strongest force in the world. . . . It gives you the winning advantage in all human contacts.[2]

Possibilities

7. Are possibilities, the what-ifs, causing fear in your life? What if the thing you fear does take place? What is the worst thing that can happen?

8. Read Psalms 112:7 and 57:7. What can you do while you are waiting and wondering about a particular situation?

Perplexities

Sometimes we don't understand why God allows certain things to happen in our lives. During these times Satan will play tricks with our minds, if we allow him.

9. How can 2 Timothy 1:7 be an anchor to hold on to during perplexing times?

Why would [God] give you something to do and no gumption to do it with? It makes no sense. So rest assured that whatever work God has for you, you are equipped to handle it beautifully. . . . There is nothing to fear. And yet, like a living Moses, I argue with God that I am not who He thinks I am. It is a pointless argument, and He always has the last word. . . . "My Spirit in you is stronger than any spirit of fear, ever. Can you believe Me?" [3]

Power, Love, and a Sound Mind

Let's take 2 Timothy 1:7 apart and see what it means to have a spirit of power, love, and a sound mind.

10. How does God give us a spirit of power (Philippians 4:13; Romans 8:31, 37)?

11. Why do we need a spirit that is confident that God loves us (Romans 8:31, 38, 39)?

12. How can we keep a sound (disciplined) mind to overcome fear
    (Philippians 2:5; Isaiah 26:3)?

God doesn't want us fearful! God doesn't want us fear-driven and fear-ridden! God wants us on top of our fears! How? By power and love and a sound mind! . . . Pace your mind by the One whose mind is the most beautiful and positive of all. Think along with Him. "Let this mind be in you which was also in Christ Jesus" (Philippians 2:5). That's healthy! That's wholesome! That's headed somewhere! [4]

The Solution to Fear

Believing God's promises is the solution to fear.

13. Do you believe God can deliver you from your fears? Why?

14. How was David delivered from his fears (Psalm 34:4)?

I can hear someone saying, "I know God can help me, but. . . ."

"What if _____ comes back?" "What if the money runs out?" "What if something happens to one of my kids?" Let's consider some what-ifs that people deal with.

15. "What if I am in danger?" Psalm 91 and Isaiah 41:10 can relieve your fear. Why?

16. "What if I feel like I just can't handle another problem?" First Corinthians 10:13 and 2 Corinthians 12:9 and 10 can relieve your fears. How?

17. "What if the way ahead looks dark and confusing?" Proverbs 3:5 and 6 can relieve your fears. How?

18. "What if I don't know what to do?" James 1:5 can relieve your fears. How?

19. What happens when we won't believe God's promises and obey them (James 1:5–8; 2 Chronicles 24:20)?

Freedom from the Fears of What-ifs

Know where your fears are coming from.

> *"Be sober, be vigilant; because your adversary the devil, as a roaring lion, walketh about, seeking whom he may devour" (1 Peter 5:8).*

Face your fears head-on.

> *"What time I am afraid, I will trust in thee" (Psalm 56:3).*

Give your fears to God.

> *"In God I will praise his word, in God I have put my trust; I will not fear what flesh can do unto me" (Psalm 56:4).*

Conquer your fears.

> *"I sought the LORD, and he heard me, and delivered me from all my fears" (Psalm 34:4).*

How is God going to deliver you from your fears? Can you bundle them up and take them to the garbage bin? No, you must conquer them one by one.

20. Make a list of the things you fear might happen—your what-ifs. Now that you have faced them, which one do you need to conquer first?

Palms-up living has helped me defuse the what-ifs with "Whatever, Lord!" and is teaching me to be content with "whatever."

 From My Heart

The first time I taught this lesson, and now again as I write it for you, I asked myself, "What is my greatest fear?" Driving on the interstate!

Normally when my husband had to fly out of the Tampa or Orlando airport, he drove the car to a park-and-ride parking lot. He left his car there, and a shuttle bus took him to the airport. As the parking fees got higher and higher, he often commented, "I don't know why you can't drive me. It sure would be cheaper."

One day I decided it was time to face my fear and conquer it. The next time J. O. had to fly, I offered to drive him to the airport and explained why. I got back to Lakeland fine and rewarded myself by going to Taco Bell for lunch. When I opened the car door after eating lunch, I saw J. O's. billfold lying by the edge of the door, ready to fall out. My first thought was, *He will not be getting on that plane without a driver's license.* So I went home to see if he had left a message on the answering machine (this was before we had cell phones). Sure enough, I had a message from J. O. By that time, he had missed his plane. I drove back to the airport and took him back again the next day. As I was driving home the second time I told the Lord, "Did You really have to make such a big deal out of this the first time I decide to face my fear?"

What are your fears? You will never conquer them until you face them head-on and start conquering them. Remember, contentment comes from our relationship to God and our confident trust in Him, not from our response to our circumstances or people. Again, we must keep putting our palms up and say, "Give what You want and take what You want."

From Your Heart

Did you write down your biggest fear? Now that you have faced it, will you work on conquering it? Where are you going to start?

Notes

   1. Lee, 102.

   2. Morgan, 108.

   3. Karon Phillips Goodman, *You're Late Again, Lord!* (Uhrichsville, OH: Barbour Books, 2002), 150, 151.

   4. Morgan, 105–107.

Learning to Be Content regardless of the If-onlys

"This one thing I do, forgetting those things which are behind, and reaching forth unto those things which are before" (Philippians 3:13).

All of us have our if-onlys, most of which are minor issues. However, some are life-changing. *If only* my husband hadn't left me. *If only* our children had listened to us. *If only* I hadn't accepted his invitation to lunch. *If only* I hadn't walked away from God.

A well-known pastor had an if-only experience that resulted in a book he titled *Rebuilding Your Broken World*. In it he described "broken-world people" as those who sustain a major blow in life, whether self-inflicted or the result of someone else's treacherous actions. These, he wrote, are some of the questions broken-world people ask: "Is there a tomorrow? Will there be another chance? Is the damage permanent? Do new starts exist? Can this broken world ever be rebuilt?"[1]

Most of the people whose worlds have been "broken" by sin deal with a common problem—guilt. The dictionary defines guilt as "the fact of having committed a breach of conduct [especially] violating law and involving a penalty."

Guilty people wish they could undo their past, but they can't. They dwell in dark valleys because they have never learned to face and resolve the problem of guilt. In addition to breaking God's law, guilt can be a feeling of blame.

Two Kinds of Guilt: Destructive and Constructive

Constructive Guilt

1. When is guilt constructive, and how do we rid ourselves of it (1 John 1:9)?

2. Read Psalm 51. What verses indicate that David was constructively aware of his guilt? Explain.

Verses 4 and 5

Verse 10

Verse 12

Verses 13 and 15

Verse 17

Destructive Guilt

3. When are feelings of guilt destructive? Why?

4. Why might believers still feel guilty after they have asked for forgiveness (Matthew 6:12, 14, 15)?

5. To be freed from guilt, forgiveness may need to be twofold. What does God do when we confess our sin (1 John 1:9)? How should we treat those who have sinned against us (Matthew 6:12, 14, 15)?

If you have confessed your sin and have forgiven those you needed to forgive, you are free. Yes, the doors of the prison you put yourself in are open—you have been freed to enjoy the abundant life God planned for you.

6. If you belong to Christ, you have all the resources you need for life and godliness (2 Peter 1:3). What are some of our resources?

Philippians 4:13

2 Timothy 1:7

2 Peter 1:3–8

I read about an elderly woman who was found in her home dead from malnutrition and exposure. In her belongings neighbors discovered stacks of

> *Social Security checks that had never been cashed.*
> *We shake our heads when we hear such accounts,*
> *not realizing that we, too, possess unused treasures*
> *and untapped resources. We have living within us*
> *Him who is able to do "exceeding abundantly above*
> *all that we ask or think" (Eph. 3:20). We have Jesus*
> *Christ in us, the hope of glory. If we will accept what*
> *He offers, we can stay on top!* [2]

You may be asking some of the if-only questions in the introduction of this lesson. Let's find some answers.

Is There a Tomorrow?

Yes, there is a tomorrow when you turn loose of the past.

7. Read Hebrews 12:1. What weight, or sin, did you have to let go of to be freed from the guilt of your past?

8. Read Philippians 3:13 and 14 and Luke 9:62. Why must we let go of the if-onlys of the past?

> *Some there are that torment themselves afresh*
> *with the memory of what is past; others, again,*
> *afflict themselves with the apprehension of evils to*
> *come; and very ridiculously both—for the one does*
> *not now concern us, and the other not yet. . . . One*
> *should count each day a separate life.* [3]

Will There Be Another Chance?

Yes, there will be another chance. God does not keep a record of our failures. "I will forgive their iniquity, and I will remember their sin no more" (Jeremiah 31:34).

9. Who got another chance after he failed miserably and could have lived a life of regret and guilt (Matthew 26:30–34, 69–75)? Why was he forgiven (John 21:1–17)?

Peter learned a good lesson from his failures, but he didn't continue to wallow in a pit of despair and guilt. Christ reminded him that He knew where Peter had been but that He was far more concerned about where Peter was going and what He had for him to do.

Is This Damage Permanent?

No, damage does not need to be permanent; we can start over again.

10. The prodigal son had to lose everything before he came to his senses. Why did he think he would still be welcomed back into his father's home (Luke 15:17–24)?

11. Have you been a prodigal child, or do you have a prodigal child? What is needed to heal the damage (Ephesians 4:32)?

If a parent forgives an estranged child, does that parent have to open up to be hurt again? Not necessarily. A parent can forgive all of his child's

> *past behavior and still refuse to let that child move*
> *back into the house. We can forgive a child and not*
> *loan him money again. Forgiveness doesn't mean*
> *we surrender our sense of safety. We might forgive*
> *an embezzler and yet not make him president of the*
> *bank. We might forgive an alcoholic and still refuse*
> *to buy him alcohol. Parents can forgive and still be*
> *reasonably cautious, careful, and even watchful.*[4]

Do New Starts Exist?

Yes, a new start is possible; however, sometimes we have to start down a new path.

12. Paul was sincere in his religion, but he was going down the wrong path. What had to happen to get him to leave that path (Acts 9:4–6; 16:25–31; 26:1–21)? How did he change?

13. Are you heading in the wrong direction? If so, which of these paths are you on? Are you religious but lost? Do you, like the apostle Paul, need Christ as your Savior? If so, read Romans 10:9, 10, and 13 and ask the Lord to save you.

14. Are you a believer who is walking away from God? Do you need to turn around and walk with Him? Will you?

15. Why do people resist a new start with God (Jeremiah 7:24)?

Today is a new day. You will get out of it just what you put into it. . . . If you have made mistakes, even serious mistakes, there is always another chance for you. And supposing you have tried and failed again and again, you may have a fresh start any moment you choose, for this thing that we call "failure" is not the falling down, but the staying down.[5]

Can This Broken World Be Rebuilt?

Yes, God can restore and rebuild our lives when we are truly repentant and want to make a new start.

16. David was a broken-world person. What two sins did he commit that caused him extreme pain and guilt (2 Samuel 11:3–5, 14–17)?

17. How did David feel before and after he confessed his sins (Psalms 32; 51)?

18. David didn't lose his salvation when he sinned. What did he lose that needed restoration (Psalm 51:1–4, 12)?

19. David was totally honest and repentant about his sin.
    According to Acts 13:22, how does God remember David?

Remember, we are not failures if we fall; we are failures if we don't get up and try again. You can have an abundant life after failure because God is a God of starting over. He puts new life into withered and dried hearts.

Have your if-onlys dried and withered your heart and robbed you of contentment? Why don't you let go of them all, put your palms up, and say, "Lord, give what You want and take what You want." You won't be sorry!

 ## *From My Heart*

As I wrote this lesson, many friends came to mind. Some are living as victors, and some are living as victims of their if-onlys. They are born-again believers and have the same resources available to them, but only the victorious ones are using the resources available to them in Christ. Those who are living as victims are like the elderly lady who didn't cash her Social Security checks.

We all have if-onlys we wish had never happened—but they did! When they come back to haunt us, we must remind ourselves, "I am forgiven, and I will not relive my failures; that is a closed door."

We have every resource we need for life and godliness. In every situation we face, we can say, "For this I have Jesus." I am often reminded of a statement Ian Thomas made, "If you are born again, all you need is what you have, and what you have is what He is!" I have to keep reminding myself that Christ doesn't just give me strength—He is my strength!

From Your Heart

Is your world broken by sin? Are you living as a victim or as restored and victorious? What one thing in this lesson helped you most?

Notes

1. Gordon MacDonald, *Rebuilding Your Broken World* (Nashville: Thomas Nelson Publishers, 1988), 25.

2. Matilda Nordtvedt, *Living beyond Depression* (Minneapolis: Bethany Fellowship, Inc., 1978), 95.

3. Seneca, quoted in *Light from Many Lamps*, ed. Lillian Eichler Watson (New York: Simon and Schuster, 1951), 217.

4. William L. Coleman, *Parents with Broken Hearts* (Grand Rapids: Fleming H. Revell, 1996), 86.

5. Mary Pickford, quoted in *Light from Many Lamps*,158.

Learning to Be Content with the Whys

"O Lord, how long shall I cry, and thou wilt not hear! even cry out unto thee of violence, and thou wilt not save! Why dost thou [show] me iniquity, and cause me to behold grievance?"
(Habakkuk 1:2, 3).

We've all lived long enough to know that life is tough and sometimes doesn't make sense. Have you ever said, or heard another believer say, "Lord, this isn't fair; all I've ever tried to do was live for You and serve You. Why is this happening?"

If God is a God of love, why is there so much suffering in the world? Why do the wicked seem to prosper? Why do terrible things happen to nice people? Why does life have to hurt so much? Isn't there an easier way to grow? Can any meaning be found in suffering. ... Christians have no tidy answers to suffering, no easy ten principles for happy sufferers. They only have attitudes for meeting it, handles for overcoming it, outlooks for transcending it.[1]

I am learning to be content with God's dealings in my life without having to know why, because I have also learned that a major barrier to contentment is the feeling that God isn't fair.

1. How do you measure fairness?

2. When you read about the attributes of God in the Bible, is fairness ever listed as part of His character? What word do we see often in Psalm 136? Choose three of the following references to read: Job 37:23; Psalm 89:14; Proverbs 3:33; Isaiah 9:7; 45:21; Zephaniah 3:5. What characteristic of God do they show?

> *"Fairness" reduces God's standards to the place where we can perform and function in life without utter, total dependence on Him. . . . Since God isn't "fair" as humans perceive "fairness," what is the alternative? Could we please have a drum roll? Now for the good news: God is actually merciful and just. . . . Justice reveals God's true nature of love and, at the same time, reveals the rebellious nature of man, which is placed on exhibit. Therefore, justice establishes guilt when God's standards in His Word are violated. . . . This is where mercy comes riding in as our knight in shining armor. Through the eyes of mercy, He looks beyond our faults and sees our needs, patiently viewing us as finished products—even while we are in process. Mercy is given to those who agree with God's standards of righteousness, but then immediately confess their inability to achieve those standards.*[2]

At least one Bible character thought God was unfair and began to demand some answers from Him. The book of Job has more than three hundred questions, and most of them were asked by the main character, Job. It is interesting to note that God never answered any of Job's questions but began hurling questions at him (Job 38—41). After hearing God asking him questions about His greatness and power, Job realized how foolish he was to debate with the Almighty God of the universe (Job 42:5, 6).

In this lesson we will look at two other Bible characters who had questions that God never answered. They, like Job, came to realize that they didn't need to know why; they needed to know who—Who was in control of everything, including their lives.

Habakkuk's Whys

3. Habakkuk had some whys. What was one of them (Habakkuk 1:1, 2)? (Hint: This question does not start with "why." Reword it as a "why" question.)

4. Have you asked God why He is not answering your prayer? If so, what have you been praying?

5. When God did answer Habakkuk's prayer, His answer seemed almost unbelievable and left Habakkuk with a bigger why. What did God say He was going to do (Habakkuk 1:5–11)?

6. What was Habakkuk's next why (Habakkuk 1:13)? (Hint: "Wherefore" is the same as "why.")

7. Have you ever had a why similar to Habakkuk's? If so, what was it?

God sometimes gives unexpected answers to our prayers. This, more than anything else, was what really startled Habakkuk. For a long time God does not seem to answer at all. Then, when he does

> *answer, what he says is even more mysterious than his apparent failure to listen to our prayers. . . . Scripture teaches us that God sometimes answers our prayers by allowing things to become much worse before they become better. He may sometimes do the opposite of what we anticipate. He may overwhelm us by confronting us with a Chaldean army. Yet it is a fundamental principle in the life and walk of faith that we must always be prepared for the unexpected when we are dealing with God.*[3]

8. God didn't answer Habakkuk's question. How did Habakkuk respond to God's silence (Habakkuk 2:1)? What is significant about the words "I will watch to see"?

9. When we don't understand what God is doing and if we keep our eyes fixed on His promises instead of our problems, what will be the result (Psalm 57:7; Isaiah 26:3; Philippians 4:7)?

In Habakkuk 2:1–20 God told Habakkuk He was going to raise up the Chaldeans, or Babylonians, to chasten Israel but that the Chaldeans' greatness would be short-lived. He planned to give the Chaldeans the power to destroy, but they would be so proud of their power that God would raise up another power to destroy them.

Habakkuk 3:1–15 records Habakkuk's talk with God. Habakkuk asked for mercy for the people. He then rehearsed in his mind the great things God had done in the past. In Habakkuk 3:16–19 we see a man filled with fear and faith.

10. How did Habakkuk express both fear and faith (Habakkuk 3:16–19)?

Verse 16

Verses 17–19

11. How do we get the strength to live out Habakkuk 3:19 when we don't think God is fair (Philippians 4:13; Isaiah 40:31; Hebrews 4:12)?

The Christian … may "rejoice in tribulation" and be triumphant in the midst of the worst circumstances. That is the challenge of the Christian position. Herein we as Christians are to differ from the world. When hell is let loose, and the worst comes to the worst, we are to do more than "put up with it" or "be steady." We are to know a holy joy and manifest a spirit of rejoicing. We are to be "more than conquerors," instead of merely exercising self-control with the aid of an iron will.[4]

---

12. What did you learn about the whys of life from Habakkuk?

Asaph's Whys

Psalm 73 is the psalm of a discouraged man. Asaph had a why that confused him: Why do the godly suffer, when the ungodly seem to be prosperous and seem to get off scot-free? Asaph worked out the problem in his mind and came to the right conclusion—which he started with, "God is good." After recording his conclusion, he told how he had come up with that answer.

13. The perplexed psalmist was at the point of despair. Why is the edge of despair a dangerous place to be (Psalm 73:2; 1 Corinthians 10:12)?

14. Why might Asaph have been embarrassed as he looked back on what had caused his despair (Psalm 73:3)?

> *During the worst point of [Asaph's] struggle, he became convinced that living for God wasn't worth it. The reason? People who deserve to suffer, don't. People who don't deserve to suffer, do! God's moral universe seemed to be broken, with no apparent attempts by God to fix it, which in turn caused Asaph to doubt His goodness.*[5]

15. The psalmist admitted he was about to go down in despair. What thought kept him from falling (Psalm 73:1)?

16. Why must we believe God is always good—even when He doesn't seem good (Psalms 27:13; 34:8; John 10:11; Romans 2:4)?

17. When are we the most and least likely to say, "God was so good to me"?

    Most likely

    Least likely

18. Asaph's thoughts about God, recorded in Psalm 73:4–14, imply that he thought God was unfair. How do we know he was only thinking and not speaking aloud to others (vv. 15, 16)?

19. Why is it important to talk to God, not to people (except, perhaps, to a few close, mature friends), when we are perplexed and discouraged?

> *When you are uncertain and perplexed, the thing to do is to try to find something of which you are certain, and then take your stand on that. It may not be the central thing; that does not matter. [Asaph] saw the consequences of what he was about to do, and he knew for certain it was wrong. Therefore he said, "I will not say it." He is still not clear about the main trouble, but he is clear about that.*[6]

20. Where did Asaph go to get his thinking straightened out (Psalm 73:17)? Summarize the thoughts in verses 18–28 that brought him back to his remark in verse 1.

Asaph struggled big time to reconcile what he knew in his heart with what he saw with his eyes—and we often do too!... It's hard to maintain a Steady-Eddie kind of faith when we see our pagan neighbors grow rich and sassy while we try to keep the wolf from the door.... So we understand Asaph's close encounter with spiritual disaster. We totter on the same brink when we take our eyes off God's providence and fix them on our pagan neighbors' prosperity.... Time spent alone with God gave Asaph a new perspective on life. He saw that others might have gold for a while, but He had God forever (v. 23).[7]

Learning to live a palms-up life has helped me to give the whys to God and replace the whys with, "Whatever, Lord."

From My Heart

As I wrote this lesson, my mind went back to a Bible study my husband and I wrote a few years ago titled *How to Stay Sane When Life Doesn't Make Sense.* I would like to quote a thought from the introduction of that book that has helped me many times when the whys of life start causing me to feel confused and stressed: "Why? Why? Why? We know God's Word is true. And we know that God never fails, but sometimes life just doesn't make much sense to us. We want everything to make sense; we want logical answers to our questions. Would we bear our trials any better, or would the suffering seem less intense if we knew why? Probably not! If we knew why, could we keep something bad from happening? Probably not!"[8]

Rather than asking *why,* we should ask *how.* "How can I trust God is this situation?" The "whys" of life will always be difficult to understand; God asks us to trust Him, the Who of life. Charles Spurgeon said, "When you can't trace God's hand, trust His heart."

Life's roughest ride is on the humpback of the question mark of why.

From Your Heart

What is the biggest why in your life right now? Instead of asking God why, would you ask how: How can I trust You more so I can ask why less?

Notes

1. Joel A. Freeman, *God Is Not Fair* (San Bernardino, CA: Here's Life Publishers, 1987), 19, 20.

2. Ibid., 34–36.

3. D. Martyn Lloyd-Jones, *Faith Tried and Triumphant* (Grand Rapids: Baker Book House, 1987), 10, 11.

4. Ibid., 59, 60.

5. Igras, *Why Me?* 65.

6. Lloyd-Jones, 93.

7. James T. Dyet, *How to Handle Life's Hurts* (Schaumburg, IL: Regular Baptist Press, 2005), 9–11, 18.

8. J. O. and Juanita Purcell, *How to Stay Sane When Life Doesn't Make Sense* (Schaumburg, IL: Regular Baptist Press, 1999), 7.

Learning to Be Content with God's Will

"And be not conformed to this world: but be ye transformed by the renewing of your mind, that ye may prove what is that good, and acceptable, and perfect, will of God" (Romans 12:2).

God wants us to know and do His will. The big question is, Do we want to know and do His will? Many Christians fear the will of God, believing God will ask them to do something that will make them miserable. At one time in my life I was fearful of God's will. However, I have learned that God wants to make us feel marvelous, not miserable. He wants to give us a life full of purpose and fulfillment—the abundant life. God does not make it difficult for us to know His will, we do.

Most often we ask for God's will in our lives for guidance and direction regarding decisions we need to make. There are two prerequisites for knowing God's will. Let's look at them.

Prerequisites for Knowing God's Will

1. According to Matthew 7:21, who will enter Heaven? What is God's will for every person (2 Peter 3:9)?

2. After repentance and salvation, what is God's will for every one of His children (Romans 12:1)?

> *A heart of submission and dependence is crucial when looking for guidance from the Lord. Lewis Sperry Chafer, founder of Dallas Theological Seminary, said, "His leading is only for those who are already committed to do as He may lead." Alan Redpath, the great Bible teacher of an earlier generation, said, "Don't expect God to reveal His will for you next week until you practice it today."* [1]

3. Romans 12:1 and 2 present three requirements for knowing God's will. What are they?

Verse 1

Verse 2a

Verse 2b

4. How is God's will good, acceptable, and perfect (Romans 12:2)?

Good

Acceptable

Perfect

After we have met the two prerequisites for knowing God's will (salvation and a total yieldedness to do God's will), how do we find God's will as we make decisions for our lives?

Most day-to-day decisions are easy. They do not require a great deal of thinking or praying. We just do what is expected and required. Occasionally, however, we face a decision in which we don't know for sure what to do. We need God's wisdom, help, and guidance because we want His will, not ours, to guide us in the process of finding an answer. For decisions like these, we have resources available to help us. Let's talk about them.

Resources to Help in Decision-making

Scripture

5. How can God's Word help us in knowing God's will (Psalm 119:105, 130; Proverbs 3:5, 6)?

The Word of God gives us "light" for the steps we take and "understanding" as we make decisions.

The Bible is full of many commands and instructions for most of life's decisions. The more we know of God's Word, the more certain we can be of God's will. As examples, the Bible makes it clear that we are to not murder, not commit adultery, not lie, cheat, or steal, not lust, or covet. We are to forgive others, work hard, be honest, love our neighbor, give to the poor, honor parents, help others in need, not take a fellow Christian to court, and so on. . . . If any decisions violate the principle of Scripture, they are wrong decisions.[2]

> *Never expect to be guided to marry an unbeliever, or*
> *elope with a married person, as long as 1 Corinthians*
> *7:39 and the seventh commandment stand! . . . The*
> *Spirit leads within the limits which the Word sets,*
> *not beyond them. "He guideth me in the paths of*
> *righteousness"—but not anywhere else.*[3]

Prayer

6. How can prayer help us to know God's will (Jeremiah 33:3;
   James 1:5, 6)?

God answers prayer when we "ask in faith."

Counsel

7. Where should we seek our counsel and why (Psalm 1:1; Proverbs 11:14)?

> *James Packer once said, "Don't be a spiritual Lone*
> *Ranger; when you think you see God's will, have*
> *your perception checked. Draw on the wisdom of*
> *those who are wiser than you are. Take advice." That*
> *is good advice. Even when you think you have not*
> *yet seen God's will, ask advice. It's the wise thing*
> *to do. Many other people will have insight that you*
> *might not have had. Use it!*[4]

Circumstances

8. Psalm 37:23 says, "The steps [and, by implication, the stops]

of a good man are ordered by the LORD." How do circumstances often help us know God's will?

The "Fleece"

9. God told Gideon that He was going to use him to lead in the destruction of the Midianites (Judges 6:11–40). However, Gideon didn't believe God could really do that. What did Gideon do (Judges 6:37–40)? What does this test tell us about Gideon's faith?

Questions We Can Ask Ourselves

As we use the resources of God's Word, prayer, counsel, circumstances, or the fleece, we can ask ourselves questions to help us discern God's will about the decisions we need to make.

10. Read 1 Corinthians 6:12. What question could you ask after reading this verse?

11. Read 1 Corinthians 10:23. What question can you ask based on this verse?

12. Read Hebrews 12:1. The word "weight" means "needless bulk." What question comes from this verse?

13. Read 1 Peter 2:16. What question might you ask after reading this verse?

14. Read 1 Corinthians 8:9. What question do you see in this verse?

15. Read 1 John 2:6. What short question would this verse create?

16. Read 1 Corinthians 10:31. We see the basis for another short question in this verse. What is it?

17. If you have sought God's will to the best of your ability and still are unsure of God's will and direction, what should you do (Psalm 27:13, 14)?

> *"Wait on the Lord" is a constant refrain in the Psalms, and it is a necessary word, for God often keeps us waiting. He is not in such a hurry as we are, and it is not His way to give more light on the future than we need for action in the present, or to guide us more than one step at a time. When in doubt, do nothing, but continue to wait on God. When action is needed, light will come.*[5]

18. If you can't wait any longer to make your decision, and if you are not absolutely sure what to do, what course of action should you take (Proverbs 3:5, 6)?

> *When he was crossing the Irish Channel one dark starless night, says Dr. F. B. Meyer, he stood on the deck by the Captain and asked him, "How do you know Holyhead Harbor on so dark a night as this?" He said, "You see those three lights? Those three must line up behind each other as one, and when we see them so united we know the exact position of the harbor's mouth." When we want to know God's will there are three things which always concur: the inward impulse, the Word of God, and the trend of circumstances! . . . Never start until these three things agree.*[6]

Learning to be content with God's will is daily a reminder in my life as I put my palms up and remind myself and the Lord, "I want Your will more than my will."

 ## *From My Heart*

A palms-up life does not always help me discern God's will, but it is a great help in accepting God's will for my life. When I can say, "Give what You want and take what You want" and really mean it, I have great peace for what God has for me.

Knowing and doing God's will is pretty easy when He brings me out of darkness into light. However, I have learned that His same guidance can take me out of light into darkness. That's when I must bow in His presence and acknowledge that He knows what He is doing even though I don't have a clue what's going on. The darkness tends to cause me to fear until I lift my eyes and palms heavenward and again repeat, "Give what You want and take what You want. I want Your will more than my will."

Ladies, that's the secret of contentment: palms-up living.

From Your Heart

What did you learn in this lesson about discerning God's will for your life? Have you been resisting God's will in some area of your life? If so, why?

Have you given the palms-up life a try? Try it, you'll never be sorry, because it will definitely lead you down the path to contentment.

Notes

1. Max E. Anders, *30 Days to Understanding the Christian Life* (Brentwood, TN: Wolgemuth & Hyatt, Publishers, 1990), 323.

2. Ibid., 322, 323.

3. J. I. Packer, *Knowing God* (Downers Grove, IL: InterVarsity Press, 1973), 215.

4. Anders, pp. 324, 325.

5. Packer, 217.

6. Cowman, 20.

Leader's Guide

Suggestions for Leaders

The effectiveness of a group Bible study usually depends on two things: (1) the leader herself; and (2) the ladies' commitment to prepare beforehand and interact during the study. You cannot totally control the second factor, but you have total control over the first one. These brief suggestions will help you be an effective Bible study leader.

You will want to prepare each lesson a week in advance. During the week, read supplemental material and look for illustrations in the everyday events of your life as well as in the lives of others.

Encourage the ladies in the Bible study to complete each lesson before the meeting itself. This preparation will make the discussion more interesting. You can suggest that ladies answer two or three questions a day as part of their daily Bible reading time rather than trying to do the entire lesson at one sitting.

You may also want to encourage the ladies to memorize the key verse for each lesson. (This is the verse that is printed in italics at the start of each lesson.) If possible, print the verses on 3" x 5" cards to distribute each week. If you cannot do this, suggest that the ladies make their own cards and keep them in a prominent place throughout the week.

The physical setting in which you meet will have some bearing on the study itself. An informal circle of chairs, chairs around a table, someone's living room or family room—these types of settings encourage people to relax and participate. In addition to an informal setting, create an atmosphere in which ladies feel free to participate and be themselves.

During the discussion time, here are a few things to observe.

• Don't do all the talking. This study is not designed to be a lecture.

• Encourage discussion on each question by adding ideas and questions.

• Don't discuss controversial issues that will divide the group. (Differences of opinion are healthy; divisions are not.)

• Don't allow one lady to dominate the discussion. Use statements such as these to draw others into the study: "Let's hear from someone on this side of the room" (the side opposite the dominant talker); "Let's hear from someone who has not shared yet today."

• Stay on the subject. The tendency toward tangents is always possible in a discussion. One of your responsibilities as the leader is to keep the group on track.

• Don't get bogged down on a question that interests only one person.

You may want to use the last fifteen minutes of the scheduled time for prayer. If you have a large group of ladies, divide into smaller groups for prayer. You could call this the "Share and Care Time."

If you have a morning Bible study, encourage the ladies to go out for lunch with someone else from time to time. This is a good way to get acquainted with new ladies. Occasionally you could plan a time when ladies bring their own lunches or salads to share and eat together. These things help promote fellowship and friendship in the group.

The formats that follow are suggestions only. You can plan your own format, use one of these, or adapt one of these to your needs.

2-hour Bible Study
10:00—10:15 Coffee and fellowship time
10:15—10:30 Get-acquainted time
             Have two ladies take five minutes each to tell some-thing about themselves and their families.
             Also use this time to make announcements and, if ap-propriate, take an offering for the babysitters.
10:30—11:45 Bible study
             Leader guides discussion of the questions in the day's lesson.
11:45—12:00 Prayer time

2-hour Bible Study
10:00—10:45 Bible lesson
             Leader teaches a lesson on the content of the material. No discussion during this time.
10:45—11:00 Coffee and fellowship
11:00—11:45 Discussion time
             Divide into small groups with an appointed leader for each group. Discuss the questions in the day's lesson.
11:45—12:00 Prayer time

1½-hour Bible Study
10:00—10:30 Bible study
             Leader guides discussion of half the questions in the day's lesson.
10:30—10:45 Coffee and fellowship
10:45—11:15 Bible study
             Leader continues discussion of the questions in the day's lesson.
11:15—11:30 Prayer time

Answers for Leader's Use

Information inside parentheses ( ) is additional instruction for the group leader.

LESSON 1
1. As restless, troubled people with no peace.

2. A person has peace with God when he or she accepts by faith what Jesus Christ did on the cross for his or her sin. He shed His blood to take away our sin.

3. (Read the verses and then ask for a response.)

4. The *Webster's New World Dictionary* (1968 ed.) defines "sovereign" as "supreme in power, holding position of ruler."

5. *Proverbs 16:9*—God directs our steps. *Ecclesiastes 7:13*—God's works are perfect, even if He made them "crooked." *Psalm 115:3*— God does whatever He pleases, with whom He pleases, and when He pleases. *Daniel 4:34, 35*—No one can change or thwart God's will. He works out every event to accomplish His will. *Lamentations 3:37, 38*—God determines whether we can do what we have planned.

6. He is the "blessed and only" Sovereign, the "King of kings," and "Lord of lords."

7. Personal answers.

8. He viewed God as the "most High" and the inhabitants of the earth as nothing in His sight. He saw God as the ruler of Heaven and Earth; no one could stop or question His power and authority to rule. He realized God had broken his proud spirit.

9. A God who pops up when needed. The thinking behind a jack-in-the-box view of God is, "Don't call me, I'll call you."

10. God doesn't think and act like we do. What this means in practical terms is that many of our questions—especially those that begin with the word "why"—will have to remain unanswered for the time being.

11. When evil occurs, God permits it and uses it for His glory. He can make even human wrath praise Him.

12. Job said the Lord gives and the Lord takes away.

13. Job did not know why God allowed his trials, but he did come to understand God's might and power over his life and all of His creation. He also finally understood that he didn't need to know why; he just needed to trust the Almighty God.

14. To decide what should be done or what is right or wrong.

15. A righteous and holy God Who always does what is right.

16. (Ask for discussion from the group.)

17. (Ask a volunteer to share her experience.)

18. How will this situation help conform My child to the image of My Son, Jesus Christ?

19. Here is my explanation of a palms-up life. I open my palms before God and say, "Lord, give what You want and take what You want." Palms-up living is the opposite of living with clenched fists, afraid of what God might send or take.

20. God is going to give or take what He chooses with or without our permission. Our response can lead to acceptance and peace or to kicking and screaming.

LESSON 2

1. (Ask the ladies to share their thoughts.)

2. "The substance of things hoped for, the evidence of things not seen."

3. The Word of God.

4. That Christ died, was buried, and rose again to pay for my sins.

5. *1 Corinthians 16:13*—Stand in the faith. *2 Corinthians 5:7*—Walk by faith. *Galatians 2:20*—Live by faith.

6. By sight.

7. Her faith is immature. She needs spiritual food to grow, yet she's not ready for meat (the deep things of God). A new believer is able to handle only the milk (the basics) of the Word.

8. Double minded; up and down; unstable.

9. Habakkuk, Job, and Jeremiah.

10. Their confidence in God. They knew God was doing something in their lives even though they couldn't always see or understand what it was.

11. (Ask the ladies to take this self-exam.)

12. (Lead the group in discussing their answers.)

13. Because He is in control of everything. Our spiritual good.

14. Because we are in His hand.

15. (Lead the group in discussing their answers.)

16. God's Word will not fail or pass away. It will endure forever.

17. In the difficulties of life, we can ask God for wisdom.

18. (Ask the group to share some of their answers.)

LESSON 3

1. "I have learned."

2. Contentment does not come automatically as a gift to us when we are born again. It is something we enjoy as we grow in our relationship with Christ and learn to apply His promises to our daily lives.

3. (Have several ladies read their answers.)

4. He had learned to get by with only the necessities of life.

5. He was content when he had plenty to eat or not enough to eat.

6. No, because he didn't claim to do "all things" in his own strength but in Christ's strength.

7. The strength we receive from Christ sustains us.

8. (Have several of the ladies share their answers.)

9. By waiting upon the Lord, or spending time with Him in Bible study and prayer.

10. *Verse 11*—Keep us from sin. *Verses 49–52*—Comfort us. *Verses 65–67*—Keep us from going astray. *Verse 105*—Give light for guidance. *Verse 130*—Give us understanding. *Verses 161–164*—Fill our hearts and mouths with praise.

11. We can't learn to be content in our own strength. We need the strength we gain from God's Word to be content in every situation.

12. They tell us that everything God allows is for our spiritual good.

13. (Ask a few ladies to share their thoughts.)

14. (Ask a few ladies to share their thoughts.)

15. It reminds us to forget the past and press to the future with our

eyes on Christ instead of on our circumstances.

16. We should not dwell on tomorrow but keep focused on today.

17. We have enough problems to deal with each day without borrowing problems that don't exist.

18. (Have a few ladies share their thoughts.)

19. (Answers may vary.) Remember, we can't do this in our own strength. We must learn to draw upon Christ and the Holy Spirit for strength.

LESSON 4

1. I can find something to be thankful for in every situation that I am in.

2. Nothing can touch my life that God does not allow. Therefore, that thing becomes God's will for me.

3. Our God is loving and forgiving, but He is also just and righteous. When we knowingly violate God's commands (e.g., Exodus 20:14), we are asking for His chastening or correcting (Hebrews 12:5–11).

4. "Always" and "all." It is hard to thank the Lord for the bad things He allows that seem to make no sense. Yet we know that everything He allows is ultimately for our spiritual good (Romans 8:28, 29).

5. Four times (in verses 8, 15, 21, 31). God wants us to be grateful for His goodness and for His works to us.

6. (Ask the ladies to share some of their complaints and thanks.)

7. God was displeased and angry. He is never pleased with a complaining spirit, especially when we have so much to be thankful for.

8. Moses was miserable and felt overwhelmed because of their constant complaining. He wished he could just die. He might have used a term we often hear: "I'm sick to death of you." Our complaining can make other people miserable and cause them to not want to be around us.

9. If we think unbiblical thoughts, we'll have unbiblical feelings. We cannot feel discouraged unless we are thinking discouraging thoughts. If we think Biblical thoughts, we will feel joyful and contented.

10. We must learn to "cast down" our ungodly and discouraging thoughts.

11. We must imprison the unbiblical thoughts that are running around in our minds. This means we must not give them the freedom to control our minds.

12. So that we'll be obedient and pleasing to Christ. When God gives us a command, He expects us to obey it!

13. Things that are "true."

14. Tomorrow is not real because it has not happened yet.

15. The past is gone; it cannot be changed. What is real is what is happening today. Today's events are the only ones we can deal with and change.

16. *Psalm 103:13 and 14 and 1 John 1:7–9*—God has realistic expectations of believers. He knows our weaknesses. He knows we will sin, but He forgives us when we do. *Psalm 130:1–8*—God forgives completely and

totally. *Isaiah 40:11*—God is compassionate enough to carry us when we are too weak to go on. *1 Samuel 16:7*—God is more concerned about our hearts than about our appearances. *Jeremiah 31:3*—God loves us unconditionally—when we succeed and when we fail. *Psalm 91:14–16*—God will never abandon believers; He is our security. *1 Peter 5:7*—God wants us to bring everything, every care, to Him.

LESSON 5

1. Christ suffered an agonizing death on the cross to pay for our sins.

2. He forgives our sin, blots it out, and doesn't remember it.

3. We keep rehearsing their sin so they can't forget how much they hurt us.

4. Love them and do good to them.

5. He works in us so we want to forgive, and then He gives us the strength to do it.

6. (Ask a few ladies to share their experiences.)

7. No one deserves or can earn God's forgiveness. It is all of grace.

8. God is the One Who keeps score, and if they need to pay, He will do it in His time and in His way.

9. They attack the person who caused the broken relationship rather than the problem that caused it.

10. Trying to win back an offended person is like trying to capture a fortified city. Anger and hurt are as hard to get past as barred gates. Trying to win back an offended person takes much time, effort, and prayer. But the pain will be worth the gain if you succeed.

11. He showed us He loved us. By sending His Son to die for our sins, He took the first step in making peace with us and in showing us that love. We then must take the initiative to make things right with Him.

12. Everlasting, or unconditional. Conditional love responds in kind. Unconditional love responds with love—even when mistreated.

13. "He humbled himself." Christ set aside His rights and placed our needs above His.

14. Pride. It is so hard for us to humble ourselves.

15. Suffering, misunderstanding.

16. (Ask a few in the group to share their experiences.)

17. Jesus instructed us believers to invite the other individuals to talk about the issues so that the differences can be resolved. We can forgive without trying to restore the relationships. However, broken relationships cannot be mended without inviting reconciliation and talking about the problems.

18. Because Christ keeps forgiving us, we must keep forgiving other people.

LESSON 6

1. Worry is crossing bridges before we reach them.

2. Unstable—up and down. Trusting God one day and not trusting Him the next day.

3. *Younger women*—Money, children, finding a mate, marriage, job, or career. *Older women*—Retirement, health, children, grandchildren, losing a mate. *All women*—Everything!

4. When God says, "With [Me] nothing shall be impossible" and we say, "God can't," we call Him a liar.

5. A disease is "a condition of the living . . . body or of one of its parts that impairs normal functioning and is typically manifested by distinguishing signs and symptoms." A disease makes us sick and can be destructive. Worry is destructive to our mental health. It is different from most real diseases because it is self-imposed and because it is a sin.

6. Extremely ridiculous. We can't even add an inch to our height by worrying, so what good does it do? None.

7. We do not know what plan God has in mind for us and if tomorrow will even come.

8. Make our plans but be ready to adjust if God changes our plans.

9. He tells us He will meet all our needs.

10. Personal answers.

11. God is intimately involved in what is happening in our lives. He knows about every detail and cares about every need.

12. God is all-powerful and has promised to help us with all of our struggles and fears. It is unwise to worry about something God is already taking care of.

13. Worry can cause heart trouble, high blood pressure, headaches, and a host of stomach disorders.

14. What has already happened can't be changed. Worrying about it is a waste of time and energy, a senseless task, like sawing sawdust.

15. We know we shouldn't do it. Does saying, "Everyone does it" make it right? No. God tells us not to worry about anything.

16. *Verse 4*—Rejoice in the Lord, not in your circumstances. We can't always rejoice in what God is allowing, but we can rejoice in the fact that He is in control of what He is allowing. *Verse 5*—If you treat others with moderation, you won't have to worry about your actions. *Verse 6*—Turn every care or worry into a prayer. *Verse 7*—Be thankful that God is in control of what is happening. *Verses 8 and 9*—Think on Biblical, godly things and obey God's Word. *Verse 10*—Think about others. Quit worrying about your problems and try to help someone else with his or her problem.

17. *Verses 11 and 12*—Accept what God is allowing without resentment. *Verse 13*—Draw upon God's power in you to do what you know you should do.

18. Believe God can and will supply all your needs, not your "greeds." We often think God isn't supplying our needs because we mix up our wants and our needs.

LESSON 7

1. "Self-image."

2. "Self-esteem," "self-worth."

3. We know we have been transformed because God says so and because we see ourselves changing. We love new things, and we put away the old things of the flesh.

4. They don't put off their old habits and ways of thinking.

5. We will always feel that we're too fat or too thin, that we don't exercise enough or don't eat the right food. Nothing is as perfect as the pictures I constantly see and the messages I hear everyday on TV and radio.

6. God is concerned with inward beauty (1 Peter 3:3, 4).

7. God views outward beauty as vain. This implies that the woman who focuses on outward beauty is also vain.

8. (Personal answers.) We often let the world set the standard for our beauty.

9. The beauty of the Lord.

10. A woman who needs these things is in bondage to them. She expects from them what she can receive only from God.

11. God's everlasting love.

12. He loves us unconditionally, no matter what we do.

13. Friends.

14. All things.

15. We can't do it, but Christ can change us because He lives in us. We have supernatural power in us now.

16. Wisdom from God.

17. We walk in the light, not darkness. We have been redeemed; our sins have been forgiven.

18. Power, love, and a sound mind.

19. It is our fault because we yield to the flesh (our old nature) instead of yielding to the Holy Spirit.

20. We no longer live by fleshly thoughts or what the world is telling us. We now have the mind of Christ. We are trying to view ourselves and life from God's perspective.

LESSON 8

1. Living on the amount of money you make. Living on a budget so you know how much you make and how much you spend. If you can't pay off your credit card when the bill arrives every thirty days, you are living outside your box.

2. The lust of the flesh, the lust of the eyes, and the pride of life.

3. (Ask a few ladies to share their answers.)

4. (Personal answers.) Ask yourself if there is anything in your life you would not be willing to give up if God asked you to.

5. How we spend our money indicates which we love the most: the Lord or our money.

6. You don't have to have a bigger house, a more expensive car, or more things just because your income increases.

7. Credit card offers.

8. Food, clothing, a place to live. All the basics we need for life.

9. No. God is talking about the heart. These things should not be used just for our pleasure but for God's glory and to bless and help others.

10. Agur's heart was in the right place; he served God, not things. He would be satisfied with "just enough."

11. He blessed the Lord because he knew it all belonged to God and that He could give or take as He chose.

12. Our things are not what life is all about.

13. "Not rich toward God." If we are "not rich toward God," or spiritually rich, none of our material riches will allow us to enjoy the happy, contented life God wants us to experience.

14. Godliness.

15. The same way—with nothing in our hands.

16. The word "raiment" in verse 8 is "covering." Food to eat, shelter to protect our heads, and clothes to warm our bodies are enough to keep us content.

17. Money tempts us to be trapped by the places it can take us. We can experience pressures to sin that someone with less money will never know. The love of money can lead to our ruination and destruction.

18. No, money is just a piece of paper or metal. Money is no more evil than a nice big steak. What is evil, or what we should hate, is living for it and loving it so much that we feel we never have enough.

19. When people love their money more than God, the things of this world are more enticing to them than serving God is! Their faith slowly weakens, and they live like the rest of the world, discontented. "Godliness with contentment is great gain (v. 6)." Ungodliness with discontentment is great loss.

LESSON 9

1. Satan.

2. Most people fear rejection or abandonment.

3. We can put our trust in God. We do not have to fear people. God is always by our side.

4. Admit you are fearful. Face your fear; don't run from it. Keep dwelling on God's promises instead of on your problem, and you'll have peace.

5. The *Merriam-Webster Dictionary* says that a phobia is an irrational fear of a particular thing or situation. When we dwell on a problem until it paralyzes us with fear, it has become a phobia. Perfect (mature) love for God and trust in Him casts out our phobias and fears.

6. We know God loves us and that nothing can touch our lives that He does not allow. When we are confident of God's love, we can approach people in a spirit of love as well.

7. (Ask a few ladies to share their answers.)

8. Keep your heart fixed on God's promises.

9. It can be an anchor by reminding us that the fear is not from God. Satan wants to play tricks with our minds.

10. Through His Holy Spirit and by our believing He is on our side. He wants us to be victors not victims.

11. We must believe God loves us and would never allow anything that would draw us away from Him.

12. We need to try to think like Christ and keep our minds fixed on Him and His power to help us.

13. (Ask ladies to share some of their thoughts.)

14. He looked to God for help and deliverance. Sometimes we ask God to help us, but we don't ask Him to deliver us from our fears.

15. God has His angels watching over believers, and He is in charge of my circumstances. He is right beside me, holding me up.

16. God will never give me more than I can bear. His grace and strength will sustain me.

17. If I trust God and not what I am thinking and feeling, He can lead me through the darkness.

18. God promises wisdom if I ask for it and believe He can give it.

19. We are unstable, and the Lord cannot bless us.

20. (Ask ladies to share some of their answers.)

LESSON 10

1. When we have sinned, we confess our sin.

2. *Verses 4 and 5*—David knew God had seen his sin, and he felt guilty. *Verse 10*—He knew God could remove his guilt and renew his spirit. *Verse 12*—He wanted God to restore the joy he had lost. *Verses 13 and 15*—He was ready to tell others what God had done for him. *Verse 17*—God did not despise David's remorse for his guilt and his sense of shame.

3. When we have confessed our sin but don't believe or live as though we are forgiven.

4. They haven't forgiven those who have caused the if-onlys in their lives.

5. Forgives us. Offer forgiveness.

6. *Philippians 4:13*—Christ, Who empowers us for everything He wants us to do. *2 Timothy 1:7*—Power, love, and a sound mind. *2 Peter 1:3–8*—His divine nature, faith, virtue, knowledge, patience, temperance (self-control), godliness, brotherly kindness, love.

7. (Ask some ladies to share their answers.)

8. We can't press forward to the goal of Christlikeness if we are always looking backward. If a plowman looked backward, the rows he was plowing would be crooked.

9. Peter was forgiven. Christ still had a ministry for Peter to do—feed His sheep.

10. He knew his father loved him and would forgive him, although he expected to become a servant, not a son.

11. The asking for forgiveness and the giving of forgiveness.

12. Christ had to save him and change his direction in life. Paul had been killing Christians; afterward, he preached so people could become Christians.

13. (Ask a few ladies to share their salvation testimonies.)

14. (Ask one or two ladies to share their experiences.)

15. They won't listen to God. They keep listening to the evil thoughts they have been hanging onto.

16. Adultery and murder.

17. Before he confessed, he was miserable. After he confessed, he was blessed and happy.

18. His joy.

19. A man after God's own heart.

LESSON 11

1. (Answers may vary.) If I do right, I should be treated right.

2. No, fairness is not listed. *Psalm 136*—Mercy. *Job 37:23*—Judgment, justice. *Psalm 89:14*—Justice and judgment. *Proverb 3:33*—Justice. *Isaiah 9:7; 45:21*—Judgment, justice. *Zephaniah 3:5*—Justice.

3. Why wasn't God answering his prayer?

4. (Ask a few ladies to share their answers.)

5. He was going to use the wicked Chaldeans (Babylonians) to chastise Judah, the Southern Kingdom, for her disobedience. (God had already chastised the Northern Kingdom, Israel, through the Assyrians, who had taken the Israelites into captivity and transported them.)

6. Why are you using a nation more wicked than us to chastise us? We are bad, but they are even worse.

7. (Ask a few ladies to share their answers.)

8. I will watch to see what God will say so that I will know what to tell the people. He was keeping his eyes fixed on God instead of on his circumstances.

9. A heart of praise and a peace that passes all understanding.

10. *Verse 16*—He expressed his fear; his belly trembled and lips quivered. *Verses 17–19*—He expressed faith; even if the fields and the flocks failed, he would still rejoice in the Lord.

11. By relying on the Lord instead of ourselves, by keeping our mind focused on Christ, and by spending time in His Word.

12. (Ask a few ladies to share their answers.)

13. Standing on the edge of despair can shake the greatest saints. They can become depressed and even have and yield to thoughts and actions that they never thought they were capable of thinking or doing.

14. He had envied foolish, ungodly people.

15. He remembered the goodness of God to Israel and to those who

want to please Him.

16. Because He says He is good; goodness is part of His character.

17. *Most likely*—We always say He is good when something good happens. *Least likely*—We have a hard time saying the same thing when bad things happen.

18. Because he wrote, "*If* I say, I *will speak* thus . . ." (emphasis added).

19. Our unbiblical thoughts could cause others to be discouraged as well.

20. God's house. Asaph realized two truths: (1) the wicked will come to an unenviable end (vv. 18–20), and (2) it was enough to have God in Heaven, which made him wealthy. Let the ungodly have their wealth; he was satisfied with his God (v. 25). Asaph found God all-sufficient. God was the strength of his life (v. 26).

LESSON 12

1. Those who do God's will to come to repentance. Each person must acknowledge that he or she is a sinner and trust Christ to save him or her.

2. God wants us to present our bodies as living sacrifices. He expects a total yieldedness of our will so we can happily do His will (v. 2).

3. *Verse 1*—Total yieldedness. *Verse 2a*—"Not conformed to this world," or to thinking and acting like the ungodly world. *Verse 2b*—Having a renewed mind by reading/studying God's Word each day and thinking godly thoughts.

4. *Good*—Best for my spiritual well-being. *Acceptable*—Pleasing to me. *Perfect*—No better way. (I have marked these definitions in my Bible beside Romans 12:2. They remind me that God's will is always for my spiritual good and that if I will accept this truth, I will see God's will as good and just right for me as well.)

5. God's Word enlightens our minds and gives us direction as we trust His promises and act on them, not on what we think is right.

6. God promises that when we ask for help and wisdom, He will give them to us.

7. We should not get counsel from the ungodly but from those who know God. Often we need counsel from others to see if they view the situation the same way we do.

8. To let us know His will, God often opens and shuts doors (that is, allows us to go, or stops us from going, a certain direction).

9. He put out a fleece twice and asked God to make it wet and then dry. Gideon's faith was weak and needed a second and third confirmation from God. God had already told him once that He would give him victory over the Midianites.

10. Will what I want to do bring me into bondage?

11. Will what I want to do edify me, or build me up spiritually?

12. What I want to do is not a sin, but is it a needless weight that will slow me down?

13. Will what I want to do hypocritically cover my sin?

14. Will what I want to do cause a weaker believer to stumble? Would I want others to imitate what I want to do?

15. Would Jesus do it?

16. Will it glorify God?

17. Wait. When in doubt, don't do anything until you are sure of God's leading.

18. Trust God to lead you with the light you have and to turn you or stop you if you are heading in the wrong direction.